Igniting King Philip's War

LANDMARK LAW CASES
&
AMERICAN SOCIETY

Peter Charles Hoffer
N. E. H. Hull
Series Editors

Titles in the series:
The Bakke *Case*, Howard Ball
Reconstruction and Black Suffrage, Robert M. Goldman
Flag Burning and Free Speech, Robert Justin Goldstein
The Salem Witchcraft Trials, Peter Charles Hoffer
The Reconstruction Justice of Salmon P. Chase, Harold M. Hyman
The Struggle for Student Rights, John W. Johnson
Igniting King Philip's War, Yasuhide Kawashima
Lochner v. New York, Paul Kens
Religious Freedom and Indian Rights, Carolyn N. Long
Marbury v. Madison, William E. Nelson
The Pullman Case, David Ray Papke
When the Nazis Came to Skokie, Philippa Strum
Affirmative Action on Trial, Melvin I. Urofsky
Lethal Judgments, Melvin I. Urofsky

YASUHIDE KAWASHIMA

Igniting King Philip's War

The John Sassamon Murder Trial

UNIVERSITY PRESS OF KANSAS

© 2001 by the University Press of Kansas

Published by the University Press of Kansas (Lawrence, Kansas 66049), which was
organized by the Kansas Board of Regents and is operated and funded by Emporia
State University, Fort Hays State University, Kansas State University, Pittsburg
State University, the University of Kansas, and Wichita State University

Library of Congress Cataloging-in-Publication Data

Kawashima, Yasuhide, 1931–
    Igniting King Philip's war : the John Sassamon murder trial / Yasuhide Kawashima.
      p. cm. — (Landmark law cases & American society)
    Includes bibliographical references and index.
    ISBN 0-7006-1092-8 (cloth : alk. paper) — ISBN 0-7006-1093-6 (paper : alk. paper)
      1. Indians of North America—Legal status, laws, etc.—New England—
    History—17th century. 2. Trials (Murder)—New England—History—17th
    century. 3. Discrimination in criminal justice administration—New England—
    History—17th century. 4. King Philip's War, 1675–1676—Causes. I. Title.
    II. Series.
    KF8205.K38 2001
    973.2'4—dc21   00-054648

British Library Cataloguing in Publication Data is available.

Printed in the United States of America
10 9 8 7 6 5 4 3 2 1

FOR MY MOTHER, AND TO THE MEMORY OF MY FATHER

CONTENTS

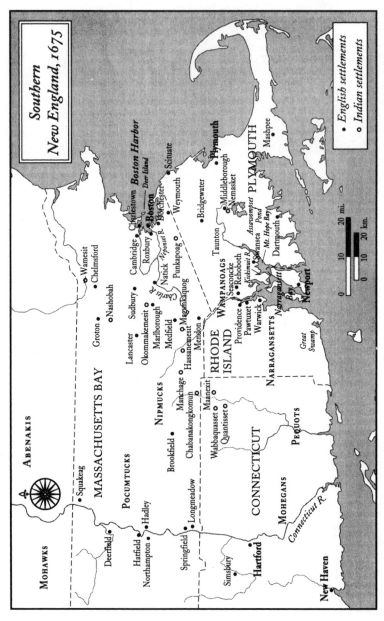

Southern
New England, *1675*

MOHAWKS

ABENAKIS

MASSACHUSETTS BAY

• Squakeag

POCUMTUCKS

• Deerfield

• Hatfield
Northampton • • Hadley

• Springfield

• Longmeadow

• Simsbury

CONNECTICUT

Hartford

Connecticut R.

MOHEGANS

New Haven

PEQUOTS

• Brookfield

NIPMUCKS

Manchage o

Chabanakongkomun •

Maanexit o

Wabbaquasset o
Quantisset o

• Groton
• Nashobah o

• Wamesit
• Chelmsford

• Lancaster

Okommakemesit o
• Marlborough

• Medfield
Magunkaquog o
Hassanemesit o
Menunkatuck o

Magunkaquog
Mendon •

RHODE
ISLAND

• Sudbury

Cambridge • Charlestown *Boston Harbor*
            Roxbury •   *Deer Island*
Natick • *Neponset R.* **Boston** • Dorchester
Punkapoag o   Weymouth • • Scituate

Charles R.

WAMPANOAGS

Taunton •

Providence •
    Pawtuxet •
Warwick •

Seaconke •
Rehoboth •

Swansea •

Kickimuit R.

NARRAGANSETTS

Narragansett
Bay

Great
Swamp

• Bridgewater

Middleborough •
Nemasket •

PLYMOUTH

Assawompset
Pond

Mt. Hope Bay

Dartmouth •

Newport •

• Mashpee

Plymouth

0   10   20 mi.

0   10   20 km.

• *English settlements*
o *Indian settlements*

Courtesy of Alfred A. Knopf, Inc.

There are some landmark law cases whose impact on American history is profound, though they appear from a distance to be insignificant. They are like the tips of vast icebergs in the North Atlantic sea lanes—almost invisible from the surface, but massive and potent—beneath it. Such a case was the murder trial of John Sassamon, a Wampanoag Indian and Christian preacher, in 1675.

Sassamon died in mysterious circumstances. He may have been killed by three of his own people for threatening to reveal to the governor of Plymouth Colony that the Wampanoag were arming for an uprising. Or the charges the colony brought against them may have been a plot to embarrass their chief, the Wampanoag sachem King Philip. Whatever actually happened, when his three councilors were brought to trial, Philip realized that the uneasy peace that had characterized colonial-Indian relations was failing. Desperate, he conceived a remarkable plan— a plan that would unite in a common cause Indian peoples who for centuries had warred on one another.

A single, simple trial of three Indians suspected of murdering a fourth Indian would forever change the way that colonists and Indians viewed one another. The outcome of the trial would lead to a civil war among the Indian peoples and a race war between Indians and colonists that ended whatever hopes Indians might have had of political independence in New England, and dashed all prospects for a truly multicultural society.

Unlike in the modern United States Supreme Court cases that other volumes in this series trace, the documentary evidence of the crime and trial here are scant and scattered. Yasu Kawashima's achievement in bringing all the evidence together and making sense of it is remarkable, but only the first of his accomplishments in this balanced and detailed account. But that is to be expected, for Kawashima is one of the foremost authorities on Indians and the law in colonial New England. To the story he brings immense learning, sympathy for both sides, and some clever detective work in medical forensics to reveal what really happened to John Sassamon.

More important still, Kawashima locates the death of Sassamon in the larger map of Indian-colonial relations, beginning with the often violent relationship among the different Indian peoples of the region. This setting serves as a backdrop for his account of the development of colonial attitudes toward neighboring Indians and Indians' views of the colonists.

Sassamon was far more than an Indian who had converted to Christianity. He not only learned and adopted the ways of the English colonists, he tutored other Indians in Christian worship and morals. For this reason, he was what the colonists hoped neighboring Indians would become. At the same time, his assimilation infuriated and frightened native leaders who wished to protect Indian ways against the inroads of colonial customs and beliefs.

The trial of the suspected murderers gave a new and (to the Indians) ominous spin to the tug of war over Indian allegiance and identity. By insisting that the death of a Wampanoag Indian, supposedly at the hands of other Wampanoags, be resolved in a colonial court, the Plymouth magistrates were announcing that the Wampanoag people could no longer employ their own methods of fact finding and retribution. The trial thus denied to the Wampanoags the last shreds of their independence as a people and a culture.

Seen in this multilayered context, the death of Sassamon and the trial of his suspected killers was of the utmost importance for the colonists and the Indians. It highlighted basic and intractable issues of identity and authority. Given its outcome, one may wonder whether King Philip's War was not inevitable. And perhaps justifiable as well? As with the iceberg, the closer we come to it, the more massive the case appears. Indeed, its implications reach to our own time, for we too have seen criminal trials whose outcome has caused large segments of our population to question one another's values, and whose outcome has led to violence.

ACKNOWLEDGMENTS

For the past four decades or so, scholars have been paying close attention to English-Indian relations in early America, especially New England, resulting in the outpouring of an unusual number of important works. This book partly relies on some of these recent studies. Not only direct quotations but various other pieces of information, views, and interpretations I have relied on are traceable in relevant books and articles cited in the bibliographical essay. I owe a special debt to the authors of these significant works.

The book is more heavily based upon my own original research conducted over the years at various research centers. I am particularly grateful to the staffs of the Huntington Library, the John Carter Brown Library, the Widener Library of Harvard University, the Massachusetts Archives, the Massachusetts Historical Society, and the Boston Public Library.

I would like to express my deep appreciation for all the help I have received on this project. Neal Salisbury provided me with many positive and perceptive comments when this work was originally conceived as a book project. Indispensable were the many penetrating questions and comments by Peter C. Mancall, who read the entire manuscript. I owe a special debt of thanks to Peter Hoffer, one of the editors of the Landmark Law Cases and American Society series, for his careful reading of my manuscript and many insightful comments and suggestions that helped improve my work substantially.

The University Press of Kansas has performed superb work, transforming my manuscript into a "salable commodity." I am grateful to Michael Briggs, editor-in-chief, who has a knack for eliciting the best work out of the author, for his patience, understanding, and encouragement. He is the kind of editor whom every author would wish to work with. Special thanks are also due to Rebecca Knight Giusti, production editor, Susan Schott, assistant director, and all others of the editorial and production staffs for their excellent work.

I am deeply indebted to the late Wilbur R. Jacobs, who made a historian out of a lawyer and gave me constant encouragement and guidance in my chosen field of English-Indian relations in early America. Alexander DeConde and Otey M. Scruggs have also always been available for advice whenever I needed it.

Finally but not least, I am thankful to my wife, Ruth Tone Kawashima, who helped me from the beginning of this project with valuable suggestions. And as always, I am deeply grateful to my parents for their whole-hearted support, encouragement, and interest.

Introduction: The Mysterious Death at the Pond

In late December 1674, John Sassamon, the minister of the Indian church at Nemasket (present Middleboro, Massachusetts) had gone to see Governor Josiah Winslow of Plymouth at his home in Marshfield. Apparently, he warned the governor that the Wampanoag sachem (New England Indian hereditary leader) King Philip (Metacom or Metacomet) was preparing for war against the English settlers and then expressed his fear for his own life.

When Sassamon did not return as expected, his friends and neighbors started looking for him but were unable to find him. Later, on January 29, 1675, a group of local Indians, who happened to be passing by Assawompsett Pond, some fifteen miles southwest of Plymouth and a few miles south of Sassamon's hometown, found a man's hat, a gun, and a brace of ducks on the frozen pond and then discovered the body of an Indian underneath the ice. They pulled the body from the water, took it to the shore, buried it there, and went hurriedly on their way.

The body was quickly identified as that of the missing Sassamon, but how did he die? To the Indians who buried the body on the shore, it looked as though Sassamon had drowned by accidentally falling into the water while fishing through a hole cut in the ice. Or was Sassamon murdered by someone from King Philip, whose activities Sassamon seems to have reported to the Plymouth governor? Did Philip actually order his men to kill Sassamon, or did some of Philip's men decide on their own to murder him without consulting their sachem?

When they heard about Sassamon's death, the Plymouth authorities, though they had dismissed Sassamon's warning as having "an Indian origin" and "can hardly be believed," immediately jumped to a conclusion that there had been foul play. They became convinced that Sassamon had been murdered. Or did Sassamon commit suicide? He had reasons to fear possible retaliation for his warning about King Philip's activities and to be depressed because his fear for his life had not been taken seriously by Governor Winslow.

Such a mysterious death needed full investigation, but who would have the right to examine the Sassamon case, and whose law, English or Indian, should be applied to it? For the Plymouth authorities, there was no question about who should handle the matter. Not only did the incident occur within the formal territorial limit of Plymouth Colony but also Sassamon, although he was an Indian, was a "Praying Indian" serving as the minister of one of the Indian churches the colony had established; thus his case should be properly placed under the jurisdiction of the Plymouth court. The area, however, was not yet settled by the colonists. It was the heart of the Wampanoag country. These Indians, moreover, may have believed that the death of an Indian should be handled by the relatives of the dead themselves, not by the English, regardless of where the incident occurred.

The death of Sassamon took place on the frontier, almost a vacant area physically but a place where the peripheries of two cultures merged, creating potentially dangerous situations based upon tension, hostility, fear, and insecurity between the two peoples. Sassamon lived his life in this flux area and in a precarious situation, playing the role of go-between for the two peoples, who held each other in mutual suspicion.

The ensuing chapters will recount the process of how this case came to be settled and how the English and the Wampanoags responded to it. The way the case was eventually resolved had profound impact not only on the Wampanoags and their neighboring native groups but on the English colonists in southern New England as well.

In order to fully understand this incident and its significance, it is necessary to grasp the case in a broad historical context of English-Indian relations in southern New England. Special attention should be paid to the nature of the merging area between the two totally different societies, the changing attitudes of the English and the natives toward each other, and the intricate relations among the different Indian groups as well as between the English and the Indians during the fifty-five year period after the founding of the first New England colony of New Plymouth in 1620.

CHAPTER I

Entangling Alliance:
The Pequot War and After

Less than seven years after the founding of the Massachusetts Bay Colony, the English colonists in New England became involved in a major military encounter with the natives in Connecticut, where the Massachusetts emigrants had recently established the towns of Hartford, Windsor, and Wethersfield on the Connecticut River. This confrontation, which came to be called the Pequot War, 1637–1638, was triggered by the murders of two English ship captains in 1634 and 1636, but its underlying causes were Puritan hostility toward the natives, trade rivalry between the English and the Dutch, and intertribal disputes among the Pequots, Narragansetts, Mohegans, and other Indian groups in the region.

Hostilities began in October 1636, when the Massachusetts authorities sent an expedition led by John Endecott to Saybrook at the mouth of the Connecticut River to exact retribution from the Pequots. They held the Pequots responsible for the two murders, but instead of settling the issue, this punitive expedition intensified the tensions between the English and the natives. The commander of the Saybrook fort, Lieutenant Lion Gardener, was outraged. "You came hither to raise these wasps around my ears," he protested to Endecott, "and then you will take wing and flee away." And so it happened. Endecott's mission did indeed place the infant Connecticut towns in grave danger. As soon as Endecott and his men left, the enraged Pequots retaliated by attacking Saybrook and Wethersfield. In response, the Connecticut General Court declared an "offensive war" against the Pequots on May 16, 1637.

The Connecticut settlers, who could not wait for aid from Boston, raised a force of ninety men and placed it under the command of John Mason and John Underhill to crush the Pequots. Realizing that their force was grossly outnumbered by the Indians in the unfamiliar enemy territory, Mason and Underhill concluded that the only way to win the war was to outmaneuver the Pequots. Instead of risking a direct attack on Weinshauks, the village of the Pequot grand sachem Sassacus, they resolved to mount a surprise attack on the Pequot stronghold, Mystic Fort.

Pretending to the Pequots that the English force was returning home by sailing from Saybrook to Narragansett Bay, Mason and Underhill landed their force on the western shore of the bay and made an overland march to the Pequot fort. After their landing on May 23, Captain Mason asked the Narragansett sachem Miantonomo for permission to cross his country. The sachem, though he sympathized with the English cause against the Pequots, thought the English force was "too weak to deal with the Enemy, who were (as he said) very great Captains and Men skilfull in War."

Miantonomo then suggested that the attack on the Pequots, who were short of supplies and therefore vulnerable, be entrusted to his warriors, with the English role limited only to providing sea transport for the striking force. Mason, however, thought the proposal dubious and stuck to their orginal plans.

The next day, the English marched westward about twenty miles to the main village of the Eastern Niantics, former Pequot tributaries, many of whom had married Pequots. The Niantics did not receive the English warmly and "carryed very proudly toward us; not permitting any of us to come into their Fort." Mason, therefore, posted "a strong Guard to be set about their Fort, giving Charge that no Indian should be suffered to pass in or out," warning the Indians at the same time that "none of them should stir out of the Fort upon peril of their Lives," in order to prevent them from going to the Pequots to warn them of the English attack.

In the following morning, a band of Narragansett warriors arrived at the village and urged the Eastern Niantics to join with them in helping the English defeat the Pequots. The Narragansetts "suddenly gathering into a Ring, one by one," Mason recorded, "making solemn Protestations how galliantly they would demean themselves, and how many Men they would Kill." The all-day march to Mystic soon began, with about five hundred Indians: Mohegans, Narragansetts, and Eastern Niantics. The soldiers suffered from heat and lack of provisions. When they had marched about twelve miles and came to a ford of the Pawcatuck River, where "the Pequots did usually Fish," the Narragansetts began to desert. Mason wrote:

> The Narragansett Indians mainfesting great Fear, in so much that many of them returned, although they had frequently despised us, saying, That we durst not look upon a Pequot, but themselves would perform great Things; though we had often tole them that we came on purpose and were resolved, God assisting, to see the Pequots, and to fight with them, before we returned, though we perished.

Mason then turned to Uncas, the Mohegan sachem, whose seventy men had remained with the English, and asked what his men would do: "The Narragansetts would all leave us, but as for Himself He would never leave us: and so it proved: For which Expressions and some other Speeches of his, I shall never forget him. Indeed he was a great Friend, and did great Servce."

They marched on, and late at night they decided to pitch the camp close to Fort Mystic, with the plan to attack the fort next morning before dawn. They could hear singing coming from the fort of the Pequots, who were celebrating English cowardice, "with great Insulting and Rejoycing," because they had seen "our Pinnaces sail by them some Days before" and "concluded that we were afraid of them and durst not come near them."

On Friday, May 26, the English overslept, due to the strenuous long march the previous day. Captain Mason recounted his story:

> In the Morning, we awaking and seeing it very light, supposing it had been day, and so we might have lost our Opportunity, having purposed to make our Assault before Day; the Indians shewing us a Path, told us that it led directly to the

Fort. . . . We held on our March about two Miles, wondering that we came not to the Fort, and fearing we might be deluded: But seeing Corn newly planted at the Foot of a great Hill, supposing the Fort was not far off.

Mason then summoned Uncas and Wequash, the renegade Pequot, from behind:

We demanded of them, where was the Fort? They answered On the Top of that Hill: Then we demanded, where were the Rest of the Indians? They answered, Behind, exceedingly afraid: We wished them to tell the rest of their Fellows, That they should by no means Fly, but stand at what distance they pleased, and see whether English Men would now Fight or not.

Captain Underhill, who had been marching in the rear, came up to join Mason. After "commanding ourselves to God," they divided their forces to enter "two Entrances into the Fort . . . at once."

Captain Mason leading up to that on the North East Side . . . heard a Dog bark and an Indian crying Owanux! Owanux! which is Englishmen! Englishmen! We called up our Forces with all expedition, gave Fire upon them through the Pallizado; the Indians being in a dead indeed their last Sleep: Then we wheeling off fell upon the main Entrance, which was blocked up with Bushes about Breast high, over which the Captain passed, intending to make good the Entrance, encouraging the rest to follow.

Captain Mason entered a wigwam, where he "was beset with many Indians, waiting all opportunities to lay Hands on him, but could not prevail." Some Indians fled, while "others crept under their Beds." Mason then went out and saw "many Indians in the Lane," who fled as he pursued. Seven of them were killed at the end of the lane by his men.

Meanwhile, at the southwest gate, Captain Underhill and his men also found their passage blocked with tree branches, which were removed by his men. Once inside the fort, both captains and their men had to fight the Pequots, who put up a fierce resistance. Underhill recounted:

> Captain Mason and myself entering into the wigwams, he was shot, and received many arrows against his head-piece. God preserved him from many wounds. Myself received a shot in the left hip, through a sufficient buff coat, that if I had not been supplied with such a garment, the arrow would have pierced through me. Another I received between neck and shoulders, hanging in the linen of my head-piece. Others of our soldiers were shot, some through the shoulders, some in the face, some in the head, some in the legs, Captain Mason and myself losing each of us a man, and had near twenty wounded. Most courageously these Pequeats behaved themselves.

Mason's original intention was not to burn the village but "to destroy them by the Sword and save the Plunder," but he changed his mind and said:

> We must Burn them; and immediately stepping into the Wigwam where he had been before, brought out a Firebrand, and putting it into the Matts with which they were covered, set the Wigwams on Fire . . . and when it was thoroughly kindled, the Indians ran as Men most dreadfully Amazed. . . . And indeed such a dreadful Terror did the Almighty let fall upon their Spirits that they would fly from us and run into the very Flames, where many of them perished.

While Mason set fire on the north side, Underhill did the same "on the south end with a train of powder." Mason and Underhill, now realizing that the fort was getting too hot for them, decided to withdraw and ordered their men to "fall off and surround the Fort; which was readily attended by all." The fire swiftly overran the fort, "to the extream Amazement of the

Enemy, and great Rejoycing of our selves." Underhill vividly described the scene:

> Many courageous fellows were unwilling to come out, and fought most desperately through the palisades, so as they were scorched and burnt with the very flame, and were deprived of their arrows—in regard the fire burnt their very bowstrings—and so perished valiantly. Mercy did they deserve for their valor, could we have had opportunity to have bestowed it. Many were burnt in the fort, both men, women, and children. Others forced out, and came in troops to the Indians, twenty and thirty at a time, which our soldiers received and entertained with the point of the sword. Down fell men, women, and children; those that scaped us, fell into the hands of the Indians that were in the rear of us . . . there were about four hundred souls in this fort, and not above five of them escaped out of our hands. Great and doleful was the bloody sight to the view of young soldiers that never had been in war, to see so many souls lie gasping on the ground, so thick, in some places, that you could hardly pass along.

In the intense firing of the English muskets, some of the Narragansett allies were killed or wounded. These casualties were the result of the Narragansetts' either being mistaken as enemies because they had not been issued yellow identification bands or being caught in a crossfire.

The destruction at Mystic Fort shocked the Indians—not only the Pequot enemies but also the English allies. They were not used to killing women and children in fighting among themselves. The Narragansett sachem Miantonomo was disgusted by the massacre. In fact, less than a month before Mystic, he had visited Roger Williams at his Providence home and secured the assurance from him that the English would not harm Pequot women and children in case of attack. Williams passed Miantonomo's concerns along to the Massachusetts Bay officials, saying that "it would be pleasing to all natives, that women and children be spared."

The scope and scale of warfare waged by the English appalled the natives, but nevertheless they were not cowed by such ruthless European-style warfare; they had to slowly adjust themselves to the new way of fighting and to grimly face the English in a similar manner in the subsequent wars.

Having completed the destruction, the English decided to evacuate the area, but—"in the enemies country, who did far exceed us in Number, being much enraged"—they soon came to encounter with some Pequots. Mason observed:

Being ordered, the Pequots came upon us with their prime-men, and let fly at us; myself fell on scarce with twelve or four-teen men to encounter with them; but they finding our bullets to outreach their arrows, forced themselves often to retreat. When we saw we could have no advantage against them in the open field, we requested our Indians for to entertain fight with them. Our end was that we might see the nature of the Indian war; which they granted us, and fell out, the Pequeats, Narra-gansets, and Mohigeners changing a few arrows together after such a manner, as I dare boldly affirm, they might fight seven years and not kill seven men. They came not near one another, but shot remote, and not point-blank, as we often do with our bullets, but at rovers, and then they gaze up in the sky to see where the arrow falls, and not until it is fallen do they shoot again. This fight is more for pastime, than to conquer and subdue enemies.

Soon thereafter, the Narragansetts, "that had stood close to us hitherto, were fallen into consultation" and decided to go home, leaving the English stranded. Underhill said:

Suddenly after their resolution, fifty of the Narraganset Indi-ans fell off from the rest, returning home. The Pequeats spy-ing them, pursued after them. Then came the Narragansets to Captain Mason and myself, Crying, Oh help us now, or our men will be all slain. We answered, How dare you crave aid of us, when you are leaving of us in this distressed condition, not knowing which way to march out of the Country? But yet you shall see it is not the nature of Englishmen to deal like heathens, to requite evil for evil, but we will succor you. Myself falling on with thirty men, in the space of an hour rescued their men, in our retreat to the body, slew and wounded above a hundred Pequeats, all fighting men, that charged us both in rear and flanks. Having overtaken the body we were resolved to march to a certain neck of land that lay by the sea-side.

Having reached the land near the sea but not seeing their expected pinnaces, the English were at a loss. As they were considering what course to take, they looked out to sea and saw "our Vessels to Us before a fair Gale of Wind, sailing into Pequot Harbour, to our great Rejoycing." The English, however, suddenly encountered some three hundred Pequots from Weinshauks. Mason led "a file or two of Men" to face the enemy, "chiefly to try what temper they were of." The Pequots fought fiercely, but soon retreated, after losing a third of their forces. The English troops were now finally able to get to the ships. Underhill, in the happy rejoining of the English forces, noted that the Narragansett Indian allies of the English, while rejoicing in the Mystic victory and admiring "the manner of Englishmen's fight," cried: "Mach it, mach it; that is, It is naught, it is naught, because it is too furious, and slays too many men."

The destruction at Mystic drastically changed the mood of the Pequots at Weinshauks. Although the Pequot fighting force, which was not crushed, still greatly outnumbered the English troops and sporadically continued to put up fierce resistance, the Mystic attack largely broke their spirit and will to fight. Some surviving Pequots fled to Long Island, while others escaped into the interior. A large party of several hundred men, women, and children led by Sassacus, Mononoto, and most of the other sachems, attempted to flee to the Hudson River valley to seek refuge in the Mohawk country. Overtaken by the pursuing English forces, many of them were killed or captured. Those captives were either taken in by the Narragansetts or sold to colonial families or the West Indies. Sassacus, Mononoto, and forty warriors, however, did reach the Mohawk country, but they were all killed. The Mohawks sent the scalps of Sassacus, his brother, and five other Pequot chiefs to the Massachusetts governor before the end of 1637. A large quantity of wampum Sassacus had carried with him in his flight is said to have contributed to the deaths of these Pequots.

Subsequently, several of the surviving Pequot sachems sought to negotiate a peace offering "that If they might but enjoy Lives, they would become the English Vassals, to dispose of them as they pleased." The English, however, refused to show any mercy to those who had actively waged war on them.

The war formally ended in September 1638, when the remaining Pequot sachems were forced to sign the Treaty of Hartford. The Pequot nation was officially declared dissolved, and even the use of the word "Pequot" was forbidden. Sassacus's followers were neither permitted to call themselves Pequots nor allowed to return to their former tribal lands.

Those Pequots who had survived the war and had not been enslaved were divided up among the Indian allies of the English. The treaty assigned 80 men and their families to Uncas of the Mohegans, 80 men and their families to Miantonomo of the Narragansetts, and another 20 men and their families to Ninigret of the Eastern Niantics. The latest archaeological finding, however, reveals totally different numbers: 200 to 300 Pequot males and their families, out of 2,000 to 2,500 survivors, were incorporated into the Mohegans living at Mohegan, while another 60 to 70 males and their families were placed in five other Mohegan villages. The Pequots numbered over 3,000 at the beginning of the war, of whom only 700 or 800 are known to have been killed. The rest joined other Indians or submitted to the English.

The English not only dealt with the enemies severely during the war but even after the war treated ruthlessly those Indians who had participated in the war and threatened colonial security. On October 26, 1639, a suspected Pequot chieftain, Nepaupuck, was arrested when he and another strange Indian came to Quinnipiac (present New Haven) to trade. He had allegedly participated both in the raid on Wethersfield, which killed on its planting field six men, three women, and twenty cows and took away two young girls, and also in the attack on an English shallop during Sassacus's flight across the Connecticut River. After being confined in stocks in jail for three days, he was brought to trial, which turned out to be "a mere farce, a nothing," was convicted of having killed Englishmen, and was condemned to death, although he denied his culpability, based upon mistaken identity. On the following day, his head was cut off alive. "The executioner," according to the official record, "cut off his head with a falchion but it was cruelly done. He gave the Indian eight blows before he effected the execution. The Indian sat erect motionless, until his head severed from his body," His head was then "pitched upon a pole in the market place," to be displayed "as a grisly lesson to his brothwer aborigines." His execution was certainly more an act of vengeance, which the natives had been accustomed to take upon their enemies, than the English way of dealing with a war criminal.

The Pequot War was essentially a conflict between the Indians and the English colonists. Although the Indians fought on both sides, the English were not divided, and no English sided with the Pequots. Surprisingly, only a very few Indian groups sided with the Pequots. In fact, the Pequots ended up fighting almost alone not only against the English, mainly Connecticut and Massachusetts, but against most of their neighboring Indians. Why were so many Indians against the Pequots? What were their specific grievances against the Pequots?

Who were the Pequots? They were intruders in the Connecticut region. Originally part of the Mohican group in the upper Hudson River region, they had broken off in the early sixteenth century and had come down the Connecticut Valley to the coast. The Pequots succeeded not only in "elbowing in" and "carving out" a new domain between the Pawcatuck and Connecticut Rivers but in splitting the Niantics, who had occupied the area. The western half became allied with the Pequots, while the eastern half, being pushed to the southwestern corner (the Pawcatuck River), came under the protection of the Narragansetts.

Although the Narragansetts and the Eastern Niantics had separate identities, they had long, close ties. The Eastern Niantics were subservient to the Narragansetts at the time of the first English settlements and fought in the Pequot War along with the Narragansetts and the Mohegans on the English side, while the Western Niantics, who became Pequot tributaries and fought on the Pequot side, suffered destruction by the colonial forces. Eastern Niantics never fused so completely with the Narragansetts as to lose their independence, but extremely close ties of kinship and marriage developed between them starting in the 1640s.

The Pequots in the lower Connecticut Valley gradually established "an uneasy hegemony" over the relatively weak Indian groups in the region, without provoking much protest among them. Formally known as Mohegan (derived from Mohican), the invaders soon earned the name Pequot ("destroyer" in the Algonquian language) for their brutal tactics. Prior to the epidemic of 1616–1619, the Pequot population was large, estimated to have been twenty-eight thousand to thirty-two thousand (six or seven Pequots per square mile), which reflects the maximum extent of Pequot political power. By the eve of the Pequot War, they had become the most hated and dreaded band in southern New England to their neighboring Indians and the English alike, although they were far weaker and much less aggressive than generally recognized. In fact, by 1633, the Pequots "had already passed their zenith" and were no longer "on the rise."

The heart of the Pequot country was located in southeastern Connecticut around the Mystic and the Pequot (now Thames) Rivers. The Pequots' political power, however, extended at times to the Connecticut River Valley and Quinnipiac on the west, to the southern parts of the vast Nipmuck country of central Massachusetts, northeastern Connecticut, and northwestern Rhode Island on the north, and to the Pawcatuck River, the western extent of Narragansett influence (the present Connecticut–Rhode Island border), on the east.

The Dutch were the first European group that came into contact with the Pequots, with whom they developed regular trade by the second decade of the seventeenth century. The control of the Connecticut River, which provided access to trade with interior New England, was the key to the exploitation of commercial potential for both Europeans and Indians. In 1633, the Dutch concluded an agreement with the Pequots, accepting the Pequot claim to the area and purchasing land on the east side of the river near Hartford (Wopigwooit), then the main Pequot settlement. The Dutch induced the Pequots to respect the peace and to allow all Indians access to the Dutch trading post.

This agreement did not last long. The Pequots were unwilling to give up their trade monopoly in the Connecticut River Valley. The dissatisfaction led to the killing of a group of Narragansett traders by Pequot warriors, prompting the Dutch to take immediate action. When the Pequot principal sachem Tatobem boarded a Dutch vessel to trade, he was captured and held for ransom. The Pequots immediately sent to the Dutch a bushel of wampum, the payment demanded for Tatobem's release. They received, instead, his dead body. The Pequots, under the new grand sachem Sassacus ("he is wild," "untamed," or "fierce"), Tatobem's son, could easily have destroyed the Dutch outpost but were not interested in ending trade. They, instead, responded by resorting to the traditional law of retribution.

Shortly after Tatobem's death in 1633, a group of Pequots, headed by Sassacus and accompanied by some Western Niantics, from whom Captain John Stone had just kidnapped two men for ransom, boarded a small trading ship anchored on the low Connecticut River and killed the captain, associate captain, and six crewmen. Sassacus personally visited Captain Stone in his cabin, and when the captain soon got drunk and collapsed on his bunk, Sassacus split the captain's head with a hatchet and threw a blanket over him. The victims were, however, English, not Dutch. The Pequots simply assumed that the Europeans in the Connecticut River region were all Dutch.

Meanwhile, the Pequots, under Sassacus, numbering at least three thousand, extended their domain from Narragansett Bay to the Hudson River, including a large part of Long Island. Sassacus at the height of his prosperity had more than twenty-six sachems subordinate to him, including the River Indians along the Connecticut River, who were placed under his protection as tributaries.

The English, on the other hand, supported the claims of the local Indians, who deeply resented the Pequot overlordship and invited the English to trade and settle in their land to provide a counterweight to the Pequot dominance in the area. Naturally, relations between the English and Pequots continued to deteriorate.

In November 1634, in order to improve the situation, Sassacus sent his delegates to Boston to negotiate for a treaty with the English. The Pequots wanted to secure trade with the English, in place of the Dutch trade at the House of Hope on the Connecticut River, from which they had been cut off, and to have the Bay Colony mediate peace with the Narragansetts. The Boston government readily complied with their requests, not only granting the Pequots full trading privileges but also agreeing to negotiate peace between the Pequots and the Narragansetts, which was quickly arranged even before the Pequot delegates left town.

The Boston government, however, demanded a huge reward for their efforts. The Pequots were willing to pay well and offered two bushels of wampum, but the Puritan magistrates declared the Pequot gift inadequate. Boston was fully aware of the wealth of the Pequots, who were regularly paid large quantities of wampum as tribute from the Montauks, whose territory on Long Island was "the center of manufacture of the best wampum." They, therefore, made an excessive demand, four hundred fathoms of wampum, forty beaver skins, and thirty otter skins, "as a condition for ratifying the treaty." The Pequot envoys had no power to accept the demand, which would impose a heavy burden on them.

The Boston government also demanded the delivery of those who were guilty of murdering Captain Stone and seven other Englishmen as another condition for peace and trade with the Pequots. In response, the Pequots argued that they had been unaware at the time that the captain and his men were English, not Dutch, and insisted that they had the right to avenge Tatobem by taking some Dutch lives. The killing of Captain Stone and his men was still a legal action to revenge the murder of their grand sachem, except for "the unfortunate matter of mistaken identity." Moreover, the Bay Colony's demand seemed unacceptable considering that Stone, a notorious smuggler and privateer and an alcoholic, was not a citizen of Massachusetts or Plymouth, had abducted two Niantics for ransom, and was killed outside the jurisdiction of the New England colonies.

In 1636, the Boston officials received news of Captain John Oldham's death. They also learned that the Pequots, who believed Boston's demand for wampum was too heavy a burden and the surrender of the murderers of Stone and others was outrageous, refused to ratify the treaty of 1634.

The Massachusetts authorities took these developments as the manifestation of the Pequots' defiance, to which they quickly reacted. The response took the form of John Endecott's expedition, which started the open hostilities, eventually leading the Pequots to devastating consequences. The person who greatly contributed to, indeed seemed almost solely responsible for, the downfall of the Pequots was, however, Uncas. In creating a distinct, independent political entity at the expense of the Pequots, he achieved considerable political power and authority during his lifetime.

Uncas's family enjoyed high status within his community, which was part of the larger Pequot confederation. Born around 1606 as the second son of the Mohegan sachem Owaneco, who married his own half-sister, Uncas was, through both parents, descended from the chief sachem of the Pequots, Nuck-quut-do-waus. Uncas's mother and his grandfather were sister and brother, aunt and uncle to the chief sachem Tatobem, and probably sister and brother of Tatobem's father, the chief sachem Wopegworrit. This would make Uncas's father, Owaneco, both cousin and uncle to Tatobem. Uncas was also related to the Narragansetts through his (paternal and also maternal) great-grandmother.

Added to this strong blood tie with the Pequot ruling family, Uncas married in 1626 the daughter of Tatobem, who was succeeded by his son, Sassacus, when he was killed in 1633. In the early 1630s, Uncas, the sachem of part of the larger confederation, was still subordinate to his brother-in-law, Sassacus.

Prior to the Pequot War, Uncas revolted against Sassacus's authority five times but failed in all, forcing him to take temporary refuge among the Narragansetts each time. One of the main causes of Uncas's rebellions was his desire to obtain hunting privileges in the Pequot country, which were granted by the chief sachems. He was, however, allowed to come back as a Mohegan sachem each time after "he humbled himself to the Pequot Sachem." His repeated reinstatements are thought to have been the result of his close kinship tie with the Pequot chief sachems and the strong support among his people. Uncas's challenges to the Pequot authority were, however, costly, reducing his political power drastically. At one time he had very little land and a small number of men, "not even enough to hold a deer hunt."

By 1636, Uncas successfully seceded from the Pequots and formally created a new band under the revived Mohegan name. The Pequots and the Mohegans now became two separate bands living in the same area, the lower Connecticut Valley—the Mohegans on the west bank of the Pequot (Thames) River (present Norwich), about twelve miles upriver from Sassacus's headquarters on the east bank of the river near its mouth (near present Groton)—but they maintained close kinship ties and a political alliance. The Mohegans, whose population in 1636 was estimated at 280 to 400, were only a twig compared with the Narragansetts, who were a great tree, so Miantonomo dismissed Uncas's band.

Uncas, as the chief of the Mohegans, who continued to be a subordinate group within the larger Pequot community, had nothing to lose and everything to gain, and shrewdly endeavored to enhance his authority and the power of his small band. The opportunity came during the Pequot War—or, more precisely, Uncas instigated the war to create the opportunity. Uncas had been inciting the English against the Pequots, and when Massachusetts and Connecticut declared war on the Pequots, he immediately sided with the colonies and fought against his own brother-in-law, Sassacus. Uncas sent a large armed force into the Pequot territory and joined the English Mystic expedition.

The war served Uncas well in advancing his ambitions. As an important ally of the English, he gained control of the Pequot country and refugees. Although the Treaty of Hartford of 1638 stipulated equal distribution of the Pequot survivors between the Mohegans and the Narragansetts (eighty Pequot men and their families each), the Mohegans actually acquired more Pequots and larger territorial gains, causing deep resentment by the Narragansett sachems.

The population of the Mohegans jumped by 1643 to 2,500, which included many Pequots who were forced to change their allegiance. By quickly filling the void left by the destruction of the Pequots, Uncas had effectively assumed Sassacus's power and prominence and became a vital force in eastern Connecticut. He, however, had to win over his new followers (who had fought against him in the Pequot War) to deal with competing bands like the Narragansetts, who resented his growing power and tried to frustrate it, and to continue cultivating his relations with the English.

Uncas continued to strengthen the close ties of mutual obligation with Connecticut that the Pequot War helped him establish. Uncas signed an agreement in 1640, giving the colony exclusive rights to purchase all of the land of his band and its tributaries, sold a large tract of land around Guilford a year later, and in 1659 decided to sell all his lands to his close friend, Captain Mason. He used the firm alliance with the English to deal with his Indian enemies aggressively. The Narragansetts especially became his archenemy.

The Mohegans and the Narragansetts, who both emerged unaffected by the epidemics of the 1620s, were both allies of the English in 1636 and 1637. It was among the Narragansetts, whose sachems were his blood relatives, that Uncas had earlier repeatedly sought refuge whenever he was expelled by the Pequots. But for Uncas, after the defeat of the Pequots the Narragansetts became the main target. Uncas continued to spread rumors among the English against the Narragansetts. The English did not always believe them but used them for their own advantage.

The Narragansetts had been the most powerful and populous group in southern New England, with a population estimated to be at thirty-five thousand to forty thousand in the early seventeenth century. They controlled a vast area from Narragansett Bay, including some islands, on the east to the Pawcatuck River on the west, and north to the Nipmucks of central Massachusetts.

The epidemic of 1616–1619, which devastated many of their neighboring bands, left the Narragansetts (and other Indian groups on the western side of Narragansett Bay) virtually untouched. The epidemics "changed the way surviving Indians thought about themselves and other Indian groups." While some Indians came to "doubt the power of local medicine people," many believed that with their burning ritual "powerful Narragansett medicine people had halted the sickness at the borders of Narragansett country."

With the Indian population decimated to the east, the epidemics left the Narragansetts and several allied communities west of Narragansett Bay positioned to play a dominant role in English-Indian relations in southern New England. The Narragansetts expanded aggressively to both east and west, occupying land west of the Seekonk River and the remaining bay islands from the Pokanokets and the Pequot land between Weekapaug and the Pawcatuck River.

Long before the coming of the Europeans, the Narragansetts had been engaging in intertribal warfare, fighting against almost every major Indian group in southern New England. They went to war with the Wampanoags to prevent them from escaping their subjection by allying with Plymouth, with the Pequots over land between their frontiers, and with the Montauks and Mohegans to avenge deaths caused by feuding. Although the Narragansetts escaped the earlier epidemic, the second major epidemic, which hit southern New England in 1633 and 1634, penetrated the Narragansett country, causing the deaths of seven hundred people.

The Narragansetts differed from the neighboring Indian groups in usually having one wife, with some exceptions. The sachem Quinnapin, for example, had three wives, including the Wampanoag squaw sachem Weetamoo, King Philip's sister-in-law. They were also known to be more civil and courteous to the English than any of the other Indians. The sachem's authority over his land and people was inherited along patrilineal lines, but not necessarily from father to son.

The system of dual-sachemship, which developed in the early sixteenth century, was unique to the Narragansetts. The pair of sachems, one older and one younger, were patrilineally related: the older sachem handling internal affairs, the younger one dealing with external politics, such as diplomacy and war. (For many years, Canonicus and his nephew Miantonomo shared the principal sachemship. After Miantonomo's death in 1643, his younger brother Pessacus, then in his early twenties, succeeded to the position, and when Canonicus died four years later, Pessacus shared the chief sachemship with Canonicus's son, Mixanno, who died in 1657. Then Pessacus maintained the sole leadership until the early 1670s, when he began to share authority with Miantonomo's younger son, Canonchet.)

In January 1622, Canonicus sent to the Plymouth leaders a gift, a bundle of arrows tied together with a rattlesnake skin, which the Pilgrims took as a challenge. Although they filled the snake skin with bullets and sent it back to the Narragansetts, Canonicus refused to accept the snake skin and sent it back. This challenge bred the fear among the Pilgrims that the Narragansetts would attack their settlement—a fear they maintained until King Philip's War.

By the early 1620s, when the Dutch started to trade with the Narragansetts, Canonicus had already been claiming Narragansett dominance in the region. Having established trade relations with the Dutch, the Narragansetts did not show much interest in trading with the English until 1631, when one of Canonicus's sons visited Boston and established formal relations with the Bay Colony. A year later, Miantonomo followed with his own visit to Boston, where he and his party were "well treated." When Miantonomo's entourage were attending the sermon, three of them left the meeting and broke into "a neighbor's house" and helped themselves to goods and food in the house, as they were accustomed to in their own village. This behavior might not have been a matter of serious concern in the Narragansett community, but the governor told Miantonomo of the incident and "with some difficulty caused him to make one of his sanapps (hench-men) to beat them, and then sent them out of the town."

Roger Williams and his fellow English, who had been banished from Massachusetts Bay, crossed the Seekonk River into the Nar-ragansett territory, acquired tracts of land from Canonicus and Miantonomo, and founded Providence Plantation, which estab-lished close, friendly relations with the Narragansetts, quickly gaining respect and influence among the natives, and became their true friends. Williams "despised their religion and found many of their customs barbarous," but he was "ready to live with them and deal with them on equal terms." Later, in 1638, when John Winthrop accused him of blindly believing and transmitting Miantonomo's lies, Williams burst out, protesting:

> Sir, let this barbarian be proud and angrey and covetous and filthy, hating and hateful, (as we ourselves have been till kind-ness from heaven pitied us, etc.) yet let me humbly beg belief, that for myself, I am not yet turned Indian, to believe all bar-barians tell me, nor so basely prsumptuous as to trouble the eyes and hands of such (and so honoured and dear) with shad-ows and fables.

After the Pequot War started, the Pequots tried to win over their old enemies, the Narragansetts, as allies. When the Mas-sachusetts authorities heard the news that the Pequot delegation was on its way to the Narrangansetts, they "swallowed their pride and appealed to the outcast Williams," urgently requesting what-ever he could do to win the Narragansetts to the English side. Williams without hesitation immediately set out to meet the Narragansett sachems. When he appeared before Miantonomo and Canonicus, Williams found the Pequot messengers already on the grounds; however, he was able to persuade the Narra-gansetts not to join the Pequots, but to become allies of the En-glish. Governor Winthrop, recognizing Williams's invaluable service, proposed that he be "recolled from Banishment," but the Massachusetts council stubbornly rejected it, making no public acknowledgment of Williams's accomplishment.

The efforts of Williams were nevertheless significant; they doomed any chance of a Pequot-Narragansett alliance, which would surely have been a serious threat to the English in New England. In retrospect, this was, however, one of the crucial decisions the Narragansetts made. By succumbing to Williams's suggestion, the Narragansetts played into the hands of the English, which led not only to the Pequots' destruction but also eventually to their own.

At any rate, siding with the English, the Narragansetts aided the Connecticut and Massachusetts armies and their Mohegan auxiliaries in their attack on the Pequot fort at Mystic in the spring of 1637 and were appalled by the ruthlessness of English warfare. Relations worsened after the English victory over the Pequots in 1637, which suddenly upset the balance of power in favor of the colonists. Nevertheless, coexistence between the two cultures, in which negotiation was the key factor, still prevailed.

The best example of mediation in the clash of legal cultures, in which all sides played equal roles, took place in August 1638, just before the formal conclusion of the Pequot War. A Nipmuck man on his way home from the Narragansetts was robbed and stabbed by Arthur Peach, a veteran of the Pequot War and a one-time servant of Governor Edward Winslow, and three other English men near the path from Providence to Plymouth. They got away with five fathoms of wampum and three coats and left the man for dead. He was found, still alive, by some Indian passersby; Roger Williams and others, who were immediately sent for, heard his testimony before he died. "The natives, friends of the slain Penowanyanquis," according to Williams, "had consultation to kill an English man in revenge," but Miantonomo as soon as he heard about it "desired that the English would be careful on the highways."

All four suspects were arrested and put in jail in Massachusetts. Through Williams, the Narragansetts demanded delivery of the murder suspects. A negotiation was held by the Indian leaders, including Miantonomo, representatives of Massachusetts Bay, and the Plymouth authorities. It was decided that the Plymouth court should try the case, on the ground that the crime had been committed within the Plymouth jurisdiction and allegedly by the Plymouth colonists. The Indians were guaranteed to "see justice done upon the offenders" by the colonial court, and they did eventually witness the execution of the three offenders, with the exception of one who escaped, instead of resorting themselves to their traditional retribution.

But the Narragansetts after the war came increasingly to feel political pressure from the English. In the Treaty of Hartford of 1638, the Narragansetts and Mohegan sachems were compelled to forget their former mutual enmity and to appeal to the English rather than seek revenge if one side wronged the other. But their mutual hostility was intensified, and the Narragansetts' relations with the English became strained as the colonies sided with the Mohegans.

For about five postwar years, rumors of Indian conspiracies against the English became rampant. In these reports, which Uncas seems to have been mostly responsible for spreading, the Narragansetts were always the key players. In September 1640, for example, an alarming rumor was started that Miantonomo had sent "a great present of wampum to the Mohawks, to aid him against the English and that it was accepted, and aid promised." A year later, another report reached Boston about Miantonomo's visit to the Montauks, whom he appealed to join him against the colonists, urging them to unite with other Indian groups, "as the English are, and say brother to one another; so must we be one as they are." Instead of supporting the Narragansetts, the Montauks betrayed them and reported the speech to the English officials.

The English policy of favoring one side over the other in intertribal conflicts is most evident in the dealings between the Mohegan sachem Uncas and the Narragansetts in the early 1640s, leading to the English attack on the Narragansetts in 1643. Such "English perfidy" must certainly have led some later native leaders such as King Philip to question the integrity of their English neighbors.

When Miantonomo asked the English whether they would be offended if he made war upon the Mohegan sachem Uncas for revenge against the latter's invasion of the Narragansetts' ally under Sequasson on the Connecticut River, the English told him that if Uncas had done him or his friends wrong and would not give satisfaction, they would leave him to take his own course. Accordingly, Miantonomo mustered a thousand men and suddenly invaded the Mohegan country and attacked Uncas's home village.

Miantonomo, who was wearing heavy English armor given him by his friend Samuel Gorton, was easily captured. The Narragansetts attempted to ransom him with a forty-pound gift, which Uncas apparently accepted. The Mohegan sachem, instead of freeing Miantonomo, handed him over to the Connecticut authorities in Hartford. Although the United Colonies Commissioners did not have clear evidence of Uncas's allegations that Miantonomo had plotted against the English, they suspected that he was guilty. They began also to realize that "Uncas cannot be safe while Myantonomo Lives." He had violated the terms of the Treaty of Hartford of 1638, requiring that intertribal conflicts be settled by the English, while Uncas not only adhered to the Treaty and English hegemony but provided valuable aid to Connecticut, the colony where his territory was located.

The commissioners thus decided that Miantonomo should die and turned him over to Uncas, instructing him to take Miantonomo out of the English jurisdiction and to kill him in the Mohegan country—humanely and without torture.

Even though Miantonomo was the sachem of the group that had welcomed Uncas whenever he sought refuge in the early 1630s, Uncas was willing to carry out the order. On the road from Hartford to Windsor, Uncas had his brother kill Miantonomo. "Onkus' brother, following after Miantunnomoh," John Winthrop wrote in his diaries, "clave his head with an hatchet, some English being present." Uncas is reported to have cut a large piece from Miantonomo's shoulder and devoured it raw, exulting, "It was the sweetest meat I ever ate. It makes my heart strong." Among southern New England Indians, human flesh was not usually part of their food intake, but some Indians did occasionally chew a bit of the flesh of a distinguished enemy they had killed. To show the Indians that they were fully backing the execution, the English sent "12 or 14 musketeers" to accompany Uncas to his home to protect him from possible retaliation.

The execution of Miantonomo caused further deterioration of the already strained Mohegan-Narragansett relations. The Narragansetts became deeply grief-stricken, mourning "continually" for a year and a half, but also became enraged and determined to seek revenge on the Mohegans for their violation of the ransom rule. In order to free themselves from further adverse decisions of the commissioners, the Narragansett sachems in the spring of 1644 submitted themselves voluntarily to King Charles I of England. The act of submission was supposedly written by Samuel Gorton and personally presented to the King by Roger Williams, who was then in England.

Based upon the act of submission, the Narragansett sachems Pessacus and Canonicus rejected the Massachusetts commissioners' summons to Boston, insisting that they were subjects of King Charles just like the colonists and that neither of them was judge of the other. The sachems demanded the Bay Colony to stay out of intertribal feuds or any other problem involving only the Indians. The king, however, was not in a position to protect the Narragansetts because in the midst of the Puritan Revolution he could not even protect himself against those rebelling against his authority. Nor did the Massachusetts authorities take such a demand seriously. The appeal was thus frustrated, and the United Colonies declared war on the Narragansetts.

What the Narragansetts were trying to do was to maintain control over their own affairs in dealing directly with Uncas, without the colonists' interference. They were always careful to avoid violence against the English and to meet all their reasonable demands, but they "could not be expected to agree to their own destruction as an autonomous nation." The English, however, under the threat of an invasion, forced the sachems to sign a treaty in August 1645, in which the Narragansetts acknowledged their culpability for various misdeeds and agreed to pay two thousand fathoms of wampum and an annual tribute for each Pequot living among them, to cede the whole Pequot country to the English colonies, and to give hostages to the English as pledges of good behavior.

While Uncas was contributing to the gradual decline of the Narragansetts' power by killing Miantonomo, he had to continue to deal with the problem of the Pequots, whose political system he had been responsible for destroying. At the end of the Pequot War, the English had intended to obliterate the Pequots, forbidding them to use the word "Pequot" and to live in their former land. Within seventeen years, however, the Pequots were allowed to re-group under their tribal name and to live in their former land.

In 1655, Connecticut established four Pequot towns, which were organized into two groups to be supervised by two Pequot "governors": Robin (Casasinamon) and Harmon Garrett (Caushawashott). The land the Pequots acquired, however, was a small portion of their homeland, and their government was not independent as before, but strictly under Connecticut jurisdiction. Most of the original Pequot territory came to be occupied by the settlers from Massachusetts, Connecticut, and Rhode Island and was also claimed by the neighboring Indian groups as hunting grounds.

Uncas was confronted with the problem of the Pequots who had been forced to live among the Mohegans but wanted to return to their native land, asserting their Pequot identity. In order to create the large Mohegan-Pequot community, in which he wanted to consolidate his political power, Uncas used many devices. To gain more support from the Pequots, Uncas, "the sachem of many wives," who had long been married to Sassacus's sister, took Sassacus's widow as his wife, then soon made a third marriage to a Pequot squaw sachem's daughter. These marriages to high-ranking Pequot women, taking place in rapid succession after the Pequot War, were "one important part of Uncas's strategy to legitimatize his claim as leader of the remnants of the Pequot communities and to thus attract Pequot refugees to his Mohegan community."

By "stealing" their wives, Uncas also used marriage as a means to punish or coerce recalcitrant Pequots. In 1647, Obochiguod, one of the Pequot leaders of New London who had been resisting Uncas's authority, placing themselves within the English settlement, complained to the United Colonies that Uncas had taken away his wife and kept her against her will. Although Uncas claimed that she was not forcefully retained, the United Colonies commissioners decided against him this time, ordering him to return her to her husband.

Throughout the rest of the 1640s, 1650s, and 1660s, the Narragansetts' relations with both the Mohegans and the United Colonies—which fully supported the Mohegans, considered them protégés, and regularly intervened in their affairs—continued to deteriorate, punctuated by rumors of conspiracies, punitive expeditions, and occasional crises. Always the Narragansetts, it seemed, were the ones unjustly put upon by the colonists. As a result, the power of the Narragansetts declined considerably, but they survived. The most important support came from Roger Williams and the officials under Oliver Cromwell's government in England.

After the execution of Miantonomo by Uncas, the Eastern Niantics always backed the Narragansetts in their challenge against the Mohegans and their protectors, the English. Increasingly from the late 1640s on, due largely to the lack of strong leaders, the Narragansetts looked for advice and leadership to Ninigret, the Eastern Niantic chief sachem and Canonicus's nephew. Rapidly emerging as the most forceful leader in the region, Ninigret often represented the Narragansetts as well as his own band in dealing with the Mohegan and the English and became, like his deceased cousin Miantonomo, a lifelong rival of Uncas. He began war against the Mohegans, but the English interfered, forcing him to sign a treaty at Boston in 1647. In renewed rumors, started in late 1647, that the Narragansetts were enlisting the Mohawks to attack Uncas and the New England colonies and that the Eastern Niantics were planning to attack the Montauks on Long Island, Ninigret came to be portrayed as the main instigator. The close alliances the Mohawks had established with the Narragansetts, Eastern Niantics, and other Indians along the Connecticut River were not just rumors. The Mohawks did in fact long maintain a firm relationship with them in order to ensure the flow of wampum from Narragansett Bay.

Meanwhile, the tributary relations the Narragansetts had long maintained with the Nipmuck bands in central Massachusetts began to crumble. Mixanno, one of the Narragansett chief sachems during the late 1640s and 1650s, had the primary responsibility of overseeing Nipmuck affairs. When he died in 1657 and was succeeded by his widow, Quaiapen (Ninigret's sister, who was also called Matantuck, the "old Queen," and Sunk Squaw), the problem started. In August 1667, she sent 126 men to raid the Nipmuck village of Quatissit (near present Thompson, Connecticut) because the Nipmucks had refused to pay the Narragansetts their regular tribute. The Nipmucks challenged the Narragansetts' authority, reporting the raid to the Massachusetts government, insisting that they as "free people" owed the Narragansetts no tribute, except goods given "in a way of love." Eventually, the Bay Colony magistrates pressured the Narragansetts into promising that if the Nipmucks were "reall and unfeigned in praying to God" and living under colony government, they would return the goods they had confiscated in lieu of tributes.

In late 1652, Ninigret visited the Dutch at Manhattan, arousing the suspicions of the English, and in the following year and again in 1659 he made war upon the Montauks in order to avenge murders of the Niantics by the Long Island Indians.

During the 1660s the United Colonies, which continued to deal with Ninigret with strong suspicion, naturally looked upon Philip with favor as they dealt with Uncas. Philip, who had become the Wampanoag chief sachem in 1662, was carrying on the traditional policy of hostility toward the Niantics as well as the Narragansetts. But by the early 1670s, the balance began to tip to the opposite side. Ninigret, who was doing everything to give the English his goodwill, fidelity, and strong support, continued to assure them that Philip's attempt at challenging the English was doomed to failure.

In the mid-1670s, the Narragansetts, with a population of five thousand, were, however, still the strongest single Indian group in southern New England. The Mohegans, who were a tiny community with a small population, could effectively challenge a large, powerful confederation like the Narragansetts simply because Uncas was able to exploit the English and win their full support and confidence in his struggle against the competing native groups. Uncas's total reliance on English allies enabled him not only to defend himself from Narragansett political and military aggression but to deal with them high-handedly. Such a policy came to be deeply resented by many other Indian groups. Uncas soon found himself isolated in his favored position among the English and alienated not only from the Narragansetts and the Eastern Niantics but also from the Pocumtucks on the upper Connecticut River and the Nipmucks, whom Uncas frequently raided in the late 1650s and 1660s. These raids often threatened to involve the colonists because most of Uncas's raids were endorsed by the English. Conversely, attempts of the other groups to attack the Mohegans were quickly discouraged by the English. In May 1657, for example, when a Narragansett sachem, Quequauenuit, Mixanno's son, had asked the Massachusetts General Court for permission to join the Pocumtucks and the Mohawks in making war on Uncas, his request was flatly turned down. During the late 1660s, however, due largely to his old age, Uncas's influence began to decline.

The man who seems to have become the role model for Uncas is the chief sachem Massasoit (Ousamequin), whose Wampanoags performed only a minor function in the Pequot War but played a crucial role in the third quarter of the seventeenth century. The Wampanoags had been usually called, until about the time of King Philip's War, the Pokanokets, named after the region where most of them lived and the chief sachems' headquarters were located. When the Pilgrims settled at Plymouth, the Pokanokets comprised a group of about thirty villages in present eastern Rhode Island and southeastern Massachusetts, south of Marshfield and Brockton.

Anthropologists recognize nine subdivisions on the mainland, four on Martha's Vineyard, and several others on Nantucket and other offshore islands. The Nausets inhabiting Cape Cod, numbering about 1,200, acted independently on many important issues dealing with Plymouth colony, even though they were considered as a subgroup of the Wampanoags. The Wampanoags' traditional friends and allies to the north were the Massachusetts. A once powerful people, they were decimated in the early seventeenth century by the plagues and tribal wars, reducing their population from 3,000 to 500 between 1615 and 1634. They, therefore, readily accepted the Puritan settlers in the early 1630s in order to protect themselves against hostile inland neighbors and were willingly converted to Christianity by John Eliot. They remained friendly and close to the Wampanoags.

Massasoit had considerable personal power over the various Wampanoag bands and their tributaries, but the 1616–1619 epidemic also struck the Wampanoags hard, though not evenly. While Cape Cod, the offshore islands, and the extreme western villages were hit lightly, the area around Paturxt (Plymouth), where the Pilgrims later landed, was completely devastated. The epidemic caused the chief sachem's power and influence to diminish, and the Wampanoags were unable to withstand attacks from their traditional enemies to the west, the unaffected Narragansetts.

The Narragansetts extended their boundaries into the Pokanokets' land, driving them to some islands in Narragansett Bay, subjected Massasoit and his band to their dominance, and assumed control over the Pokanoket tributaries, including the Nipmucks, who controlled a vast area in central Massachusetts and northern Connecticut and Rhode Island. Massasoit, who fully realized that his band with a small population could not become a powerful nation to command the respect of other native groups, shrewdly recognized the need of backing by an outside force. He immediately saw a great potential in the landing of the Pilgrims. Massasoit welcomed the English settlers and established amicable relations with them to enhance his position, using them as potential allies against his enemies, especially the Narragansetts. The Plymouth leaders, by concluding the treaty of friendship with the Wampanoags in 1621, ended up inadvertently making potential enemies among the native people without ever seeing them.

The treaty, which was renewed several times in the subsequent decades, had established a firm friendship and alliance between them. The Wampanoags' formal political submission to Plymouth and the English king during the first four decades of contact was, however, more nominal than real. It did not establish a tributary relationship, nor did it make the Wampanoags a dependent and subordinate nation to Plymouth Colony. They continued to maintain and assert their political independence.

Taking advantage of Plymouth's alliance and protection, Massasoit was able gradually to reassert Pokanoket autonomy among the Indian groups during the 1620s and most of the 1630s. During the Pequot War he became a friend of the English, as his former enemy the Narragansetts did, and after the war, he was finally able to regain independence and reestablish himself as the primary ruler of the Pokanoket confederation. Massasoit continued his policy of preserving the peace with Plymouth and using its support to consolidate his power. The Pilgrims, in turn, praised him for his friendliness and willingness to sell land to settlers.

Massasoit, by concluding the treaty of friendship and alliance with Plymouth and nominally subordinating his people to the colony, was able to secure "a maximal amount of protection at a minimal cost in autonomy." He was, in fact, the first Indian sachem in New England who recognized the importance of the English to strengthen his position against other Indian groups. Uncas followed his example and used the English effectively but in a more "groveling" yet aggressive and flagrant manner.

When he died in 1660, Massasoit was succeeded by his eldest son, Wamsutta (Alexander), who assumed the leadership only for a short time; in 1662 his younger brother, Metacom (Philip) became the chief sachem. The Pokanoket-Pilgrim friendship that had been firmly established by their father began to deteriorate rapidly as these second-generation leaders found it increasingly difficult to reaffirm friendship and alliance with Plymouth without jeopardizing their political and economic independence. The world had changed drastically since the time of their father's sachemship, and the choices available to them significantly narrowed.

Philip continued to renew his formal submission and loyalty to Plymouth whenever he was compelled to do so, and such allegiance rendered important benefits. In dealing with other Indian groups, Philip could count on Plymouth's assistance. In land disputes with the Narragansetts in 1662 and 1667, for example, Plymouth intervened and settled the issues in Philip's favor, at the same time reprimanding the Narragansetts.

By the mid-1670s, many of the Pokanoket villages on Cape Cod and Martha's Vineyard had been Christianized, but the main body of the Pokanokets was located in the Mount Hope area in present Bristol, Rhode Island. The seat of King Philip's power, this region had several villages including Montaup (near the hill) and Kickamuit (near the spring), which were under increasing political, social, economic, and cultural pressure, due to the advancing English settlement. The Pokanoket population had never been large. It is estimated to have been a little over one thousand in the early 1670s, which constituted only 5 percent of the entire southern New England Indians.

The Wampanoags were doubly jeopardized. Forced to challenge the Plymouth authorities to protect their identity and autonomy, the Wampanoags could no longer count on Plymouth's protection. They had to deal with other Indian groups, especially more powerful ones, without Plymouth's strong backing.

The Indians of southern New England had been engaging in their own struggles and conflicts long before English colonization began, and the Pilgrims and Puritans quickly discovered that such intertribal rivalries were not only ancient but often bitter. The natives had been involved in war for various reasons, such as to settle boundary disputes, extend tribal authority, avenge wrongs and insults, and resist aggression.

Southern New England was not a "peaceable kingdom," where the Indian groups could live together in harmony. Nor were they able to form a large united group, due to their mutual hostilities. Some small Indian groups, having recently been devastated by epidemic diseases, became particularly vulnerable to the intrusion of the English as well as their neighboring groups.

It was intertribal struggle as the result of mutual animosities among the Indian people that the English settlers were drawn into, inadvertently at first. The Indians were the ones who took the initiative in seeking the English friendship and protection because the Indian bands, especially weaker ones, quickly recognized the advantage of having the colonists as an ally or defender against their traditional enemies.

Before long the English found themselves deeply involved in intertribal rivalries. Their participation, moreover, drastically changed the nature of the conflicts, making them more complex and intense and their warfare more cruel and atrocious. Eventually, after fifty-five years of English settlement, the various conflicts developed into a large-scale Indian-English struggle in the mid 1670s. Although many Indians sided with the English, this war, like the Pequot War some forty years earlier, was essentially a contest between two distinct cultural groups.

CHAPTER 2

Devastating Encroachment:
English Settlements
in the Indian Country

In 1641, the Narragansett sachem Miantonomo visited the Montauk Indians on Long Island. Bringing gifts this time, "instead of receiving presents," as he had previously done, he made a speech, appealing to them to join him to form Indian unity against the English. "Otherwise," he said, "we shall be all gone shortly." He proposed that he and his allies should on one appointed day "fall on" the colonists and "kill men, women, and children, but no cows, for they will serve to eat till our deer be increased again." Why was he proposing such a drastic action against the colonists? He offered the following reasons:

> Our fathers had plenty of deer and skins, our plains were full of deer, as also our woods, and of turkies, and our coves full of fish and fowl. But these English having gotten our land, they with scythes cut down the grass, and with axes fell the trees; their cows and horses eat the grass, and their hogs spoil our clam banks, and we shall all be starved.

Although this called-for Indian unity did not materialize, Miantonomo in this speech went to the heart of the problem the Indians faced in dealing with the encroaching English settlements.

An eventual military confrontation between the Indians and the colonists in southern New England might not have been inevitable, but was certainly one of the grim possibilities that the Indians and the settlers alike may have anticipated from the early period of English colonization. The settlements the colonists established were totally incompatible with the Indian world, and sooner or later one of these irreconcilable ways of life had to prevail over the other unless firm arrangements be made for mutual respect.

In order to fully understand the impact of the English settlement on the Indians and their world, it is necessary first to examine the Indians' traditional settlement pattern and their food economy, which were integral parts of their culture and ecological consideration. We should then examine the nature of the English settlement pattern and, finally, analyze the problem of whether the Indian community and the encroaching English settlement were complementary and capable of coexistence or too competitive to allow any room for accommodation.

All the New England native peoples had their own proper domains, consisting of small, cleared lands for gardens, open swamps and densely wooded areas along streams, lakes, and rivers, where there were fishing stations, and upland forests, which were used for hunting during the winter. The New England region, except for some sections (particularly Vermont, most of New Hampshire, and the western highlands of Massachusetts and Connecticut) that were apparently not occupied by any of the Indian groups, could be divided into two general areas. Northern New England was occupied by nonsedentary Indians whose main activity was hunting, while southern New England (present Massachusetts, Rhode Island, and Connecticut) was inhabited by the semisedentary natives whose lifestyle was based upon agriculture, hunting, and fishing.

The Wampanoags on the mainland inhabited the southeastern portion of present-day Massachusetts and eastern Rhode Island, the area encompassing roughly the seventeenth-century Plymouth colony. They controlled a large territory, but as practitioners of farming, fishing, hunting, and gathering, they effectively utilized most of their land one way or another, tapping many different resources for food in different regions. The Wampanoag economic activities followed a seasonal round to exploit a variety of plentiful food supply.

From spring to early fall, the Wampanoags lived in their farming villages, some of which were located on the coast. The family houses (wigwams) were scattered along the shore and were surrounded by their planting fields. Several large coastal settlements were located on the fertile lands: Mount Hope, the seat of King Philip's power, with two important villages, Kickamuit and Montaup; Sowams, the heartland of Massasoit's domain with the governmental seat, Pokanoket; and Pocasset, a large region with the village of Pocasset headed by the squaw sachem Weetamoo, who married Philip's elder brother, Alexander.

Other farming villages were not on the coast but located in the vast interior areas along the Taunton River, and were cultivated by Indians before the settlers occupied them. Among them were Wapanucket and Titicut, both of which were within Taunton River drainage. Titicut was more extensively occupied because of its nearby fishing place.

Villages were "the centers around which Indian interactions with the environment revolved." For the Indians, the villages were not just fixed geographical areas. The Indian village had a dynamic, flexible, and plastic nature. They were communities of people whose "size and location changed on a seasonal basis," frequently but regularly "breaking up and reassembling" in response to social and ecological needs.

The planting season for the Wampanoags was late April through May, when they prepared their fields and planted corn and beans together in Indian "corn hills" and squash, pumpkins, and other vegetables in between the hills. Within four months the green corn and the first squash and beans were fit to eat, but it was not until late in September that the ripe corn was harvested.

During the summer season, the Wampanoags took short one- or two-day trips to local resource stations. Some were on the seashore, where lobsters, clams, and mussels could be harvested, while others were located inland along the lakes and rivers, such as the fishing place along the falls of the Taunton River at Nemasket (Middleborough). At these inland stations, a variety of resources, including fish, water fowl, and small game, were caught.

Late spring and early summer were also the best times to harvest all kinds of native berries, such as strawberries, huckleberries, raspberries, and currants, and wild leeks and onions. Throughout early fall, the busy work of gathering, harvesting, drying, and storing agricultural products, nuts, and berries continued.

For the southern New England Indians, corn was a major food staple, and therefore the cultivation of corn was perennial and systematic. Since it was storable, corn was regularly consumed for the full ten months following the period of green or sweet corn, which was several weeks starting in early August. After it was harvested in late September, the corn was preserved for winter use in large baskets sunk into the ground, while surplus corn was traded to the northern tribes.

The importance of Indian corn as the core of the native plant cultivation is well illustrated in the story of Canonchet, Narragansett chief during King Philip's War. He regarded the planting of corn in the spring of 1676 in the newly occupied territory in the upper Connecticut Valley as so vital to continuing the war that he risked his life. He was killed when he and his small party went back to his country, which was occupied by the enemy, to get the stored seed. Canonchet firmly believed that survival solely on the basis of hunting, fowling, fishing, and gathering, without corn, was impossible.

Once the harvests were in and stored away, the fall hunting season began. Game was not only important for food but equally valuable as a source of clothing, implements, and cordage. The southern New England Indians considered the lip of a moose a special delicacy and a beaver's tail a luxury. Deer was the most highly prized animal, and smaller animals, such as beaver, fox, and otter were also eaten but valued mainly for their pelts. Fowl were eaten and their feathers used for decoration.

Land of the Indian village was divided into family hunting grounds with definite boundaries. The hunters of each of these territories were well familiar with the plants and animals in the areas. While the old people and young children remained in the villages, small bands of hunters or single families established hunting lodges ("winter wigwams"). These lodges, which were shared sometimes by several extended families, were often located far away from the main settlements. Men, occasionally with their nuclear families, departed from their lodges for short hunting trips. As a source of meat, at a distance from the main settlement every tribe had a hunting ground or deer pasture, which was kept open and well maintained.

In the Narragansett Bay area, one of the favorite hunting spots of the Wampanoag sachems, Massasoit and his sons, Alexander and Philip, was located in present-day Raynham, Massachusetts, twenty-five miles inland, where Philip set up his hunting lodge in December 1674. It was here that just before he died John Sassamon went from his town, less than ten miles away, to see Philip. Squannacook Swamps in Rehoboth was also Philip's hunting grounds.

In actual hunting, the natives very carefully tried to conceal their presence because they had to go up as close as possible to the game to make an effective use of their bows and arrows. They disguised their bodies, imitated animal sounds and bird calls, and even used animal scents. When they set traps, the Indians were very careful as to what kind of game was caught in their traps. Realizing that very frequently the deer shrewdly avoided their traps, the Indians believed with awe that a divine power in the animals enabled them to avoid any danger. They hunted animals carefully by rotating their activities in order to conserve the resources. The Native Americans, who respected the ecology of their land, never considered the human being superior to the animals. Thus Indian hunting rituals evolved around the notion that all living things had an equal right to live in this world. They harvested these animal resources cautiously, with "rituals of atonement" and "thanksgiving." It was indeed essential for many New England Indians to pray for forgiveness, to appease the spirits of the deer, before killing.

When the hunting season was over, hunters went back to the villages, which once again became fully populated. Once settled down in their villages, they performed religious ceremonies, with dances and songs to express their gratitude for successful hunts and abundant harvest. With "wild gestures and loud noises," they danced in a circle that had a large fire in the middle. They sometimes brought out their valuable items, such as fur, wampum, and even their children on rare occasions, and threw them upon the fire, as sacrifices to "Hobbamocko" (the author of evil). During this time, the Wampanoags heavily relied upon stored foods, supplementing them with local game, especially moose. They also fished with lines on frozen ponds and coves through holes in the ice.

When the ice in the rivers broke up shortly after February, the large spawning runs of alewives and shad began, followed by the salmon, adding variety to the Indians' monotonous winter diet. The gatherings at the large falls of the rivers became major social events of the year. Between May and June was the most precarious season of the year for the Wampanoags, when stored corn and beans were running out, without new planted or wild food crops ready to be eaten.

It is estimated that, during the course of the year, a Wampanoag family traveled over one hundred miles on its seasonal rounds between the coastal village and the winter wigwam, and between the temporary resource stations and the main settlements. The Indian use of food resources carried out on a yearly basis was not a random exploitation of an assortment of isolated individual species of plants and animals. Such strategies were, in fact, the result of close observation of "the interaction of man with integrated floral and faunal associations within balanced communities." Thus the natives were fully aware that any seasonal changes in resource use could have serious consequences throughout the year.

In the Wampanoag world, access to the resources of nature was guaranteed to all the members by community land ownership and the rule of reciprocity. The Wampanoag land tenure system was based upon the principle that the community was the ultimate land authority and that land could not be alienated from the community without its approval. All members were entitled to use the land (a concept known as *usufruct*), to build wigwams, to plant, to hunt, to fish, to gather, and to collect firewood, but they could not own land individually. When someone finished harvesting his resources, the land was free for the next individual to use.

The Wampanoag sachem, as the highest-ranking official, ensured the community's usufructuary land rights and protected the land from usurpation. He or she oversaw all activities relating to land, ranging from allocating planting fields and supervising planting and harvesting to representing Indian land rights in dealings with the colonists. The sachems usually had more land under cultivation than other members, because they entertained guests in the village, contributed substantially to various feasts, and helped needy families.

Reciprocity was another convention that guaranteed unrestricted resource use. For the New England Indians, social cohesion based upon reciprocity was more important and valued than individual wealth. The sachem received "tribute" in the form of "wrecks of the sea, the skins of beasts killed in their dominions, and many like things, as first fruits, etc.," which were regarded as community gifts to the sachem in exchange for the sachem's services. Within a community, reciprocity worked to ensure that no one went hungry. If any stranger came to their houses, they would give "the best lodgings and diet" they had. If someone came when they were eating, they offered the visitor what they had no matter how little they had prepared for themselves. If they acquired any provision of fish or flesh, they shared it with their neighbors. Reciprocity was also maintained "through a complex sequence of rituals," which were often performed in elaborate ways. At the harvest festival, for example, a dancer gave all kinds of items, such as "money, coats, small breeches, knives," to the "poore" who begged for favors.

The place the Pilgrims settled in 1620 was located in the land of the Pautuxet people, part of the Wampanoag Federation, nearly all of whom had been killed by the 1616–1619 plague, as had many other Wampanoag and Massachusett Indians. The Plymouth colony was thus able to establish itself on unclaimed land with the full support of the neighboring Wampanoags, who were numerically and politically weak and were in need of a potential ally against stronger interior tribes. The diplomatic and political relationship between Plymouth and the Wampanoags, therefore, was largely amicable, but the contact between the expanding Plymouth settlement and the Indian community was not.

The competition for land between the Wampanoags and the Plymouth colonists started as soon as the Pilgrims landed, and the Wampanoags were continually forced to modify their settlement patterns, in response to the colonists' aggressive method of taking over the Indian lands. By the outbreak of King Philip's War, the frontier of colonial settlement reached the vast Wampanoag country in the southeastern part of Massachusetts and the western part of Plymouth, pushing the Indians out of their settled area.

By 1650, the Wampanoags owned only a fraction of their original territories. On the eve of King Philip's War, Philip complained that his father Massasoit had given to the English his land one hundred times larger than the land he still retained for his group. The Wampanoags were pushed either to the corners of Plymouth Colony's settlements (Assonet, Cape Cod, Mount Hope, Mattapoisett, Pocasset, and Sepican) or to the isolated interior regions, such as Betty's Neck and Towser's Neck.

Betty's Neck was part of the land at Assawompsett owned formerly by the sachem Pamontaquash, the "Pond Sachem." He willed it to his son Tuspaquin, the "Black Sachem," who married Philip's sister, and his grandson (Tuspaquin's son), Soquontamonk, alias "William." Tuspaquin later sold much of his land to the colonists during the 1660s and 1670s, but he deeded land near Masquomoh Swamp and Sasonkususett and Chippinoqutt ponds to his daughter Betty (whom John Sassamon married), so it came to be called "Betty's Neck." Towser's Neck was an upland peninsula and the site of the village of the sachem Toloson, who was an ally of Philip during King Philip's War.

In this way, the Wampanoags in many areas (such as Chachucust Neck and Wannamoisett Neck) were increasingly living on the lands they had already alienated. The alienation of the land to the colonists had a profound effect on the Indians' economic activities, because their seasonal rounds were seriously disrupted as the new owners prevented the Indians from hunting, fishing, and planting corn on their former lands, occasionally causing starvation.

The English colonists advanced various arguments to justify the dispossession of the Indians in New England. John Winthrop, the first governor of the Bay Colony, for example, using the principle of *vacuum domicilium*, maintained that the Indians, who "inclose noe land neither have any setled habitation nor any tame cattle to improve the land by. & soe have noe other but a naturall right to those countries," were not entitled to land, "not under cultivation." Only the Indian land that had been "possessed and improved by subduing" should be recognized. "If we leave them sufficient for their use," he insisted, "wee may lawfully take the rest, there being more than enough for them & us." Responding to such a view, Roger Williams defended the legitimacy of the Indian hunting grounds and argued that since the Indians "hunted all the countrey over, and for the expedition of their hunting voyages . . . burnt up all the underwoods in the countrey," they had lawful title to all of New England. Comparing the forests of the New World with the "great Parkes of the Noble men" and the king's "great Forrests in England," which "No man might lawfully invade," he criticized those New Englanders who advocated taking over the Indian land.

The colonists, however, soon came to the realization that, regardless of their rationalizations, aboriginal landholding, though crude in the English sense, was enough to assert title, and they tried to secure "very extensive rights" in the land from the Indians. Williams asserted that title to the land rested in the aboriginal owners, the Indians, and could be lawfully acquired only by purchase from them. For the settlers, land was the cornerstone for economic success and security in the New World, and securing land from the Indians was vitally important. In Plymouth and other New England colonies, settlements were made by groups of colonists, who established townships on the land they were granted by the colonial government. In this pattern, farms and livestock were privately owned; fields were annually cultivated; and domestic animals—cattle, horses, swine, and chickens—were raised in large number for milk, meat, and draft purposes.

The New England colonists quickly adopted corn as a main staple, but they introduced more familiar crops, and by the 1640s, wheat became the most important crop. The production of European grains required by far more intensive preparation of land than the growing of corn did. It has been argued that the English and the Indians both relied heavily on a land base for farming, making the core areas relatively the same for equal populations. But while the natives used the natural resources just for survival and not to deplete the supply, the colonists endeavored to enhance economic gains. The colonists, therefore, had to maintain larger fields and operate more intensively than the Indians, because they intended to sell large surpluses for profit.

The English immigrants to New England came to believe that their agricultural pattern, the intensively and extensively maintained farm with diverse crops and domestic animals, was much superior to the native farming practice. More importantly, the greatest difference between the two systems of food economy was the English reliance on domestic animals for protein intake and other purposes, compared with the Indians' reliance for similar objectives on hunting, fishing, and gathering activities, which required a larger area.

Although the Wampanoags did not feel that pressure to sell the land was especially strong for the first twenty years of the contact, the Pilgrims' demand for land grew steadily as time went on. It significantly mounted thereafter in accordance with the uncontrolled population increase in the Plymouth colony. As the Indians acquired and got accustomed to European goods, and the demands for such goods increased, fur—especially the beaver fur, which the English coveted—became an important trade good for the natives. Before the coming of the English, fur had never been traded among Indians themselves, because there had been plenty of beaver resources for the need of all the natives. As the English demands for fur increased, the Indians quickly responded by hunting indiscriminately, contrary to their traditional practice of hunting "just enough animals for the needs," causing the virtual extermination of beaver. After the fur trade rapidly declined in the 1650s, the Indians no longer had anything to trade for the goods they had become so accustomed to and could not do without.

Land, therefore, became the only major commodity left for the Indians to trade with, while it had long been the most sought after commodity for the colonists. The sachems sold land for many reasons, including their personal desire to enhance their social position by possessing many highly valued European goods. For such land sales, the sachems received a greater share of compensation than their people. Theoretically, the sachem needed the approval of the entire group to relinquish a portion of the Indian land, but very often such requirements were simply ignored. By 1675, the Wampanoags had lost a substantial amount of their land.

From the beginning, the Wampanoag land had been sought after by the Plymouth settlers, but the momentum started to increase in the 1640s. In Taunton, Massachusetts, which had been settled by the English in 1630, the settlers by the 1640s were acquiring huge portions of Wampanoag land. Governor William Bradford alone had three tracts of land taken out in a patent in 1640: one from Eastham to Brewster, the second in the area of New Bedford and Dartmouth, and a third including Swansea and Rehoboth, Massachusetts, and Barrington, Rhode Island.

In 1649, Massasoit sold 196 square miles of land called Satucket, around Bridgewater, Massachusetts, for seven coats, nine hatchets, eight hoes, twenty-nine knives, four moose skins, and ten and a half yards of cotton. Massasoit and his son Wamsutta sold in 1652 the area around Dartmouth and Acoaxet, Massachusetts, for thirty yards of cloth, eight moose skins, fifteen axes, fifteen hoes, fifteen pairs of breeches, eight pairs of stockings, eight pairs of shoes, one iron pot, and ten shillings' worth of other goods. In the following year, they received thirty-five pounds sterling for Sowams (Massasoit's principal home site), and in 1661, Wamsutta sold the area around Attleboro, upon which Philip was sued later by a Rhode Islander for 800 pounds. In 1672, Philip sold twelve square miles to Taunton for 143 pounds, which came to only less than a shilling an acre.

By selling land cheaply, the Wampanoags as well as other Algonquin groups had to sell large amounts of land for some temporary needs. This is the reason why the Wampanoags lost so much of their land base so quickly.

The Wampanoags had no trouble in finding buyers. In fact, they found themselves in a seller's market, but the prices seemed always very low. Why? From the colonists' point of view, land, especially the uncleared land of the Indians (Indians rarely sold their cultivated land), was always cheap at a time when the cost of fifty acres of land was roughly equal to the cost of the passage across the Atlantic.

But that doesn't tell the whole story. The Indians were paid little for their lands, indeed, hardly representing the true value of the land for the colonists. The Wampanoags and other New England Indians, who coveted European manufactured goods and valued them probably more than the English themselves did, usually preferred to be paid in these goods, and the colonial buyers, in turn, got by with paying them less than they would have in paying with sterling. Of course with such land sales came more important, intangible favors or perquisites in terms of the English friendship, support, and protection.

The arrangement that really served as a great incentive for the Indians to sell their land and at cheap prices was the right to plant, hunt, fish, and gather on the alienated lands, a right granted to the Indian sellers when they sold the lands. The Indians were initially unfamiliar with the European concept of land ownership, but they quickly came to understand what the land transaction would entail. Most Indians, who regarded usufruct as more important than the title itself, were willing to part with the title as long as the right to utilize the land was fully guaranteed.

In some transactions, such rights were put in writing, as in a Plymouth Indian deed of 1648, in which the Indian grantors were accorded the right to hunt and set traps. One deed even included right of access to the falls of the Taunton River for the herring run. But in most cases they were informal, oral agreements. These easements were so commonly given to the Indian sellers that whether they were specified in the deeds or not, the Indians took it for granted that these rights were automatically given to them.

In 1667, for example, a part of the Wampanoag territory known as Wollomonuppoag (present-day Wrentham, Massachusetts) was purchased by some Dedham settlers. In the following spring, they were alarmed by reports that the Indians were occupying their land, cutting wood and preparing to plant crops, and sent the town selectmen with a message to the Indians, demanding their immediate evacuation of the land. The Indians, however, simply sneered at the message. The English owners appealed to King Philip, who questioned the legitimacy of the English title but offered to grant a clear title for a down payment of five pounds, which was accepted by the settlers. Four years later, it was reported that the Indians were still utilizing the land.

The easements the Wampanoags acquired when they sold the land were in theory perpetual, and they must surely have thought these rights to be so. Many colonists, however, might probably have anticipated that there would be no Indians left in the area in the near future, so that they would never have to observe the rights granted to the natives.

As expected, the guaranteed easements quickly evaporated: not only did the settlers fail to strictly honor the grantors' rights, but the Wampanoags themselves increasingly found the rights less valuable. As the land became more densely settled, forestland turned into fields, lands became enclosed, and the game, fish, and other resources depleted, Indian livelihood, which was supposed to have been guaranteed by the easements, became endangered.

Despite their declining population, the Wampanoags did not for long retain enough good land, as the colonists seized the best farmland, meadows, and other lands. Moreover, the English land tenure affected the Indians internally, compounding Indian problems of a reduced land base. Land, which had once been a community resource, was now purchased and owned individually. As the Indians attempted to redefine their rights according to the English land tenure, new confusions and conflicts over land developed among the Indians, undermining the norms of reciprocity. In the past, the Indians had shared the natural resources freely, but by the 1660s and 1670s, there was competition for the land. As land ceased to be a common resource but could be sold and purchased by individuals, the small, immediate, or nuclear family took precedence over the community.

The English land policy also frustrated the reciprocal relations between the sachem and his or her people. The sachems began to receive less tribute due to the depleted resources. One sachem complained that his men stopped paying him their proper tribute as soon as they turned into Praying Indians and came under the supervision of the colonial government. The alienation of any Wampanoag land seriously weakened the power of both the sachems and the supreme sachems, because it reduced the size of the territorial domain for both. Not only the sachems but individual Indians began to sell the land to the settlers, confronting directly the sachems' traditional right, the right to authorize all land transactions and to represent the Wampanoags in all interactions with the colonists.

Perhaps most important, the English land tenure policies destroyed the fundamental belief that no one had the right to "own" or alienate the land because the land's resources were sacred "gifts" from the Creator. After an individual finished harvesting his or her resources and gave thanks to the earth, the land was free for the next individual to use. The English concept of individual and exclusive ownership did away with such a sacred notion of land and made land a commodity.

What specific damages did the Indians incur when their land was continually taken over by the colonists and was transformed into English settlements? Although the diet of the southern New England Indians did not change much during the seventeenth century before King Philip's War, changes in Wampanoag material culture were more pronounced in the realm of weapons, tools, clothing, and utensils. A number of English goods that the Indians came to adopt made life more convenient for them, but the demands for such goods forced the Indians to become involved in extensive land sales, severely reducing their territory in size.

The vast amount of land the settlers cleared for farms drove away the game, and settlers' lands, which became increasingly enclosed, prevented the Indians' free movement for hunting, fishing, and gathering.

English cattle and swine, being left to roam freely without being fenced in, invaded and devastated unfenced native corn fields. Cattle and pigs grazing in the peripheral areas of the English towns produced competition between domestic and wild animals for the same food resources, reducing the Indians' hunting returns. Complaints were often made by the Indians that deer became scarce because the English cattle had eaten up all the grass. As a solution they started to keep cattle and hogs themselves.

Marshes and swamps, which had provided the raw materials for native baskets and mats, were now taken over by the English for grazing their cattle. Spawning runs of various fish in the rivers and streams, on which the Indians had heavily depended, were seriously interrupted by the mill dams the English constructed.

The Wampanoags were forced to share their lands with the Plymouth settlers, but this sharing quickly turned into a competition for land, which finally ceased when King Philip's War ended, removing the barrier to colonial expansion in southern New England. During the period 1620–1676, the two economic systems proved to be incapable of absorbing radical modifications without causing serious damage to their functions. The English settlement, in which many colonists strove for profit based upon the economic system of surplus production and accumulation of wealth, grew larger and stronger as time went on, without any sign of modification or accommodation for the natives.

On the other hand, the Indian system, based upon "economic modes of underproduction and replacement consumption" conditioned by the interaction of man with integrated floral and faunal associations, was by nature not dynamic nor forceful enough to challenge the European system. The Wampanoag subsistence system, even though modified by the European way to a certain extent, could not fully cope with the New England settlement, which was founded, operated, and manned by people who positively regarded economic success and prosperity as a sign of God's favor.

For a period of fifty-five years, the Wampanoags continued to yield to the demands of the Pilgrims and Puritans. The competition for land was thus largely one-sided. The Indians did show willingness to establish accommodation, compromise, coexistence, and interdependency with the settlers. Not only were the natives forced to give up a large portion of their land, but also their lives in many aspects were seriously affected by the English influence, nearly crippling the normal operation of tribal affairs.

Nonetheless, the Indians remained Indians. They seldom fully took up the English farming patterns, although they increased corn production. Their ability to make the seasonal round for food resources was severely curtailed. In response, whether they liked it or not, many Indians came to rely more on domesticated animals for their meat supply, while the cattle they were raising on their land, ironically, ended up depleting the forage for deer herds in their hunting ground, which was continually shrinking due to land sales. Consequently, they came to practice a more sedentary way of life. The European trade goods they acquired, however, were not used to adopt the European technological and material culture system but were incorporated into their own traditional Wampanoag system. They held on to whatever was left and continued, as much as they could, to maintain their own subsistence patterns, based on the seasonal round with corn, squash, beans, nuts, fish, and deer as the main foods, and to live in their traditional wigwams.

The Wampanoags had no choice but to make substantial changes, which caused severe strains among them, but they were unwilling to accept any radical alteration that would destroy their system. The traditional Indian food economy, however, was destroyed by force. It was King Philip's War that finally decided which system should prevail.

CHAPTER 3

Fearless Defender:
King Philip and the Wampanoag World

Behind the present town of Bristol, Rhode Island, on Narragansett Bay, stands the two-hundred-foot hill called Mount Hope. It was north of the hill, at its foot, that Massasoit established his headquarters in the village Sowams. It was from here that in 1621 he, his brother Quadequina, and sixty of his warriors walked some forty miles to Plymouth and concluded with the Pilgrims the first Indian-English treaty in New England. In 1670, Mount Hope remained the same, but the Wampanoag world had changed drastically over the past fifty years. The 1660s was a very critical decade for the Wampanoags. The death of Massasoit in 1660 brought about a new type of leaders, who had a totally different outlook on their world, Plymouth, and Plymouth-Wampanoag relations.

Massasoit had not only established a firm and cordial relationship with the Plymouth colony but formed close and personal relations with some of the leading Pilgrims, including Edward Winslow. In fact, Massasoit and Winslow became so close that the sachem felt he could play an Indian joke on the Pilgrims. In 1634, Winslow went to Mount Hope to check on the situation of Massasoit, who had two years earlier fled to Plymouth when the Narragansetts tried to capture him. Winslow persuaded Massasoit to visit Plymouth and returned home with the sachem. When they came close to Plymouth, Massasoit frightened the Pilgrims by sending a runner in advance telling them that Winslow was dead "and directed him to shewe how & where he was killed: whereupon there was muche feare & sorrow at Plimoth." When they both arrived, Massasoit explained his act by saying it was an Indian custom to make them more glad of his arrival when he came safely.

Massasoit had three sons, Wamsutta, Metacom, and Taka-munna, and two daughters. The third son, Takamunna, attended Harvard's Indian College, which was chartered in 1650 and officially opened five years later in order to educate Indian boys to be ministers and teachers among their own people, but he stayed at the college only briefly. The second son, Metacom, who became the Wampanoag supreme sachem in 1662, was born around 1638, just after the end of the Pequot War.

Massasoit, then fifty-eight years old, may not have had much time to spend with the newly born baby, because he was busy conducting his normal affairs of state with Plymouth and other New England colonies. Massasoit went to Boston, taking with him eighteen beaver skins, and expressed to the Boston authorities his concern that he might have provoked them during the war, and he sued for peace, although he apparently had no cause for his anxiety. Later that year, Massasoit attended the Peach trial held at Plymouth, in which four Plymouth men were tried for murdering an Indian man. On his way home, Massasoit traveled with Roger Williams, who had testified against the accused, and stopped at his Providence house before going back home.

When Massasoit died in 1660 at the age of eighty, his oldest son, Wamsutta, succeeded him as the chief sachem. Wamsutta's wife was Weetamoo, the "Squaw Sachem of Pacasset," who inherited her sachemship from her father. Wamsutta was no stranger to the Plymouth authorities, because he had been conducting diplomacy increasingly in the late 1650s, acting as the representative of Massasoit. It seemed logical, then, that Wamsutta assume the sachemship, although Massasoit's brother could have claimed it because of the strong matrilineal tradition of passing the office to the sachem's brother.

In June 1660, in recognition of having become chief sachem, Wamsutta decided to change his name. The New England Indians had a long tradition of adopting a new name on an important occasion, and Wamsutta used the occasion to adopt an English name not only for himself but also for his younger brother Metacom. Having an English name was then popular among those Indians who were friendly with the English, particularly the Christian Indians. The Massasoit family had never been friends of Christianity, but Wamsutta was perhaps influenced by John Sassamon, a former Natick Praying Indian, who was then serving him as his secretary.

When Wamsutta asked the Plymouth General Court for English names for him and his brother, the Court enthusiastically responded, ordering that Wamsutta be called by the name of "Alexander Pokanokett" and his brother, "Philip." Alexander's regime, however, did not last long. Although he tried to continue the friendly relations with Plymouth that his father had established, the relationship quickly deteriorated.

In March 1662, when the Plymouth General Court discovered that Alexander was alienating land without selling it to the colony, it summoned him to Plymouth to explain his action. When he refused, the Plymouth government sent a force of armed troopers commanded by Major Josiah Winslow to bring Alexander back to Plymouth by force. He was interrogated at Duxbury on his suspected plot against the colony, and then left for Boston. On his way, however, he became suddenly ill with a fever and was taken to Winslow's house in nearby Marshfield. Arrangements were made to take him back to Sowams as he wished. Leaving his two sons with the Pilgrims as hostages, he returned with his wife, Weetamoo, to Sowams, where he died. Some maintained that his death was caused by his violent anger at the Pilgrims who treated him so rudely, but most of the Wampanoags, including his wife, believed that he had been poisoned.

Upon the death of his brother, Philip assumed the chief sachemship. He, like his brother Alexander, had grown up during the 1640s and 1650s, when the Wampanoag society was rapidly changing. In accordance with the New England Indian tradition, Metacom had undergone the tests of manhood, spending the winter alone in the forest with only a bow and arrow, a hatchet, and a knife to defend himself against the wolves, bears, and wildcats. He also had drunk the juice of poisonous herbs, with the medicine man standing by in case of danger, until he had proved himself immune. One of his hands was scarred from the explosion of his pistol. Metacom was a tall (taller than most of the English) and physically strong man.

King Philip had many legends associated with him, some of which surely arose after the war and should thus be treated as a bit of postwar propaganda. One of the legends has it that he could throw, with the help of the Devil, a stone across the harbor from the crest of Mount Hope to Poppasquash, two miles away.

He had fierce loyalties to his father Massasoit. He is reported to have pursued an Indian one time all the way to Nantucket Island, across forty miles of sea, because the Indian had spoken ill of Philip's deceased father. Although he eventually lost sight of the man in the dunes, Philip would not leave the island until the English gave him all the money they could collect, which came to nineteen shillings! Philip, who, like Alexander's wife, firmly believed that it was English poison, not a broken heart, that had killed Alexander, was determined to avenge his murder.

When he became the chief sachem in 1662 at the age of twenty-four, Philip moved his headquarters from Sowams to the south of Mount Hope, Mount Hope Neck (part of present Bristol). It was reported that many Indians flocked to Mount Hope to celebrate his accession, and that there was among the assembled natives "great feasting and rejoycing."

At Plymouth, on August 6 that year, Philip, together with his uncle, Uncumpowett, took the oath of loyalty to the English, to which John Sassamon and four Wampanoag sachems set their signatures down as witnesses. He also formally renewed the ancient covenant that his father had made with the Plymouth leaders, promising to keep the peace.

The new sachem had all kinds of contradictory characteristics in him: he is portrayed to have been ruthless but sentimental, wily but indecisive, noble but niggardly, arrogant but conciliatory. Philip, who has been recognized as the instigator and leader of King Philip's War, was not a terrible monster or cruel barbarian, as some of the early historians portrayed him to be, but has been considered as a man of consummate skills. He was an able and crafty leader, who fully recognized the proper function of the sachem. He also had elements of human kindness, which was at times extended to the English colonists.

King Philip's personal idea of leadership, which he strictly adhered to, was based upon the persuasive ability of rulers among the New England Indians and was extended even to certain settlers who had been friendly or kind to him. Even a few days before the outbreak of the War, he invited settlers to retrieve their stray horses, although some Wampanoags were hostile and pointed guns at them when they came to the Indian camp. He also sent a canoe up Mount Hope Bay to warn his close friend Hugh Cole to flee before it was too late, a favor that could have turned out to cost Philip the war if Cole had warned his fellow Englishmen.

Then he let the war begin, though he is said to have thrown himself weeping to the ground as he gave the command. He must have felt a strong resistance to picking up arms against Plymouth, without whose protection, so Richard Harris once reminded him, his father's head would have been cut off by the Narragansetts in 1632.

Philip, who was related through blood or marriage to many Wampanoag sachems, skillfully cultivated such relations to strengthen cohesion within the Wampanoag. Weetamoo, the squaw sachem of the Pocassets, was Philip's sister-in-law not only because she married his brother but also because he married Weetamoo's sister, Wootonekanuske. Weetamoo returned to her own people after Alexander's death and married one Petonowowett, but she divorced him when he did not support Philip. Later she married one of the influential Narragansett sachems, Quinnapin, creating a new friend out of a traditional enemy.

Philip's sister, Amie, married another Wampanoag sachem, Tuspaquin (also called "Old Watuspaquin" and the "Black Sachem") of Nemasket, who supported Philip in the war until the very end. Philip's younger brother, Takamunna, thirteen years his junior, was given a separate sachemship when he reached maturity in 1671 and was totally committed to the cause of his elder brother. The supreme sachem was also able to maintain, through his craft and power, solid relationships with other influential sachems such as Awashonks of Sakonnet, Corbitant of Mattapoisett, who once wanted to ally with the Narragansetts against

Massasoit, and Coneconan (or Quachattasett) of Manomet. Awashonks, however, had been very reluctant to join Philip in the ensuing war, but was finally "threatened" into rendering him her support.

Another important method Philip employed to elicit support from sachems of Wampanoag villages or other groups was to invite their young warriors to special dances, where they would be inspired and infected by the enthusiasm of his men and would in turn influence their own sachems.

Perhaps Philip's most significant achievement was his ability to organize various bands and confederations into a unified group, which had never been done before. To unify New England Indian groups, which were by nature independent, autonomous, and self-reliant, for a common purpose required an exceptional talent. King Philip was the only one who was able to lead almost half of the entire population of New England Indians against the English colonists, though his war lasted just a few months.

He used a variety of tactics and skills to achieve his objectives: ties of consanguinity and affinity, promises, persuasion, bribery, and threats. He was also an effective strategist who made use of ambushes and raids against the enemy to arouse the warriors' enthusiasm and morale on an intertribal basis. His ablest men were sent to faraway places, trying to enlist the support of the Mohawks, French, and Canadian Indians, but this attempt proved unsuccessful.

Above all, his ability to solicit aid through persuasion seems to have been his special gift, although he was by no means always able to convince others. For example, Philip failed to entice John Sassamon to help in enlisting support from the Praying and other pro-English Indians. Occasionally, his persuasion became so aggressive that some sachems accused him of threatening them to get their support and loyalty instead of their voluntarily following him because of admiration and belief in the causes.

There was, of course, disaffection among these chiefs and their men who had been compelled to become involved in the war by Philip's arts. One of them, a Nipmuck sachem, attempted to kill Philip and threatened that he would, declaring that Philip had involved them in the war and brought great trouble upon them. Nor did Philip succeed in getting complete support even from the Wampanoags. "Capt. Amos," who refused to follow Philip and joined the pro-English Indians, fought against him as the commander of the Cape Indians.

No evidence exists to prove that Philip was a fighting warrior or that he ever participated in battles or led any attack, raid, or ambush in person. While dispersing his nonfighting people among various groups to protect them, he kept a sufficient bodyguard with him to inspire respect and ensure a bearing among the various Northern tribes. To be sure, he planned and directed many of the most bloody and destructive attacks upon the English settlements, but he seems always to have been at a safe distance from personal danger.

He did have a great ability to quickly slip away, keeping his force intact. The secret retreat of his whole active force over water from Mount Hope, leaving only one hundred women and children behind, and his narrow but daring escape from the Nipsachuck swamp into the Nipmuck country were not just due to the English failure to act promptly. It was the result of Philip's clear perception of the situation and movement of the English forces and his ability to take advantage of their weaknesses in the most effective way.

King Philip was not a strong political leader in the European sense but an effective sachem, who seems to have well understood the sachem's authority and power. He did have by upbringing and training many qualities, talents, and skills that were essential for an Indian leader. He was fiercely independent, assertive, eminent, righteous, dedicated, yet reserved, and acted more like a level-headed but shrewd negotiator than a dynamic, powerful ruler.

Except for his role in King Philip's War as the sole instigator, his accomplishments as the Wampanoag supreme sachem remain obscure. Was it that he was not truly a great tribal leader or that the exercise of his talents was hampered by the critical changes taking place within the Wampanoag society as well as in the English-Wampanoag relations?

Massasoit and King Philip as chief sachems confronted totally different problems. During the first thirty years or so, the relationship between the Wampanoags and the Pilgrims was peaceful and friendly. The Indians provided many things the colonists wanted: land, friendship and alliance, trade, and legal autonomy. The colony, on the other hand, respected the Wampanoags as an independent political entity, and therefore Massasoit could deal with Plymouth effectively by just exercising his power as the supreme sachem of the Wampanoags. The Plymouth colony was small and weak and needed friendship and alliance, and the policy founded on this weakness developed into a very amicable English-Indian relationship.

From the early 1660s on the relationship began to change drastically. As the Plymouth colony grew in size and power and became more independent, its friendly relations with the Wampanoags remained useful but no longer indispensable. Plymouth now began to conduct its business with Philip on its own terms, demanding of him more things in a more aggressive manner, less respectful of the Wampanoag tradition. The colony was exacting from Philip more than he could do as the chief sachem, unless he ignored the limit of the proper power of the sachem.

If Philip did not comply because it was beyond his capacity as the chief sachem, the Plymouth authorities took it as defiance. If Philip, on the other hand, was merely exercising his sachem's power, which might turn out to be against the policy of the colony, he was declared aggressive. How did King Philip specifically deal with these problems as the Wampanoag chief sachem?

In the transition of authority after Massasoit's death, no serious shuffling and reshuffling of territorial affiliation took place among Massasoit's followers. Philip was able to maintain the same relations Massasoit held and exerted the same loyalty from the old sachems as Massasoit did. But in actuality he ruled the sachemship with the population much decreased and territory considerably reduced and under stronger English influence.

The Wampanoag land, which was held in common and usually included village sites, fields, fishing stations, and hunting grounds, could not be alienated except through the sachem or recognized leaders after consultation with the group. The selling of tribal land, which had started during Massasoit's rule but accelerated during the rules of Alexander and Philip, often was done without consulting with the group. In 1662, for example, an Indian accused Alexander of selling land that was not his to sell. Land sales, which not only reduced the size of the Wampanoag domain but depleted the natural resources, in turn greatly weakened the bond between the sachem and his people; Philip had less land to allocate to his followers, and his subordinate sachems and their men had less tribute to give to him, an important source of income for the sachem. Philip, quite naturally, had to sell more land, making himself less dependent on his own people. Mutual dependency between the sachem and his people was completely lost in the process.

While Plymouth demanded Philip not to convey lands without its consent, he not only protested against Plymouth's practice of granting lands to the settlers near his territory but insisted that his treaty did not pledge the subjection of his people to Plymouth, but to the English king only. As if to sanction Philip's claim, the new Rhode Island royal charter in 1663 included King Philip's home of Mount Hope within Rhode Island's jurisdiction, which Plymouth naturally challenged.

In 1667, Plymouth established the town of Swansea on the frontier of Plymouth colony, an area with overlapping claims by King Philip and Rhode Island. This move greatly angered Philip, and when Philip made threatening moves near Swansea in 1671, Plymouth responded by levying a fine on him, ordering him to surrender all the arms held by his people, and authorizing Swansea's further expansion. In September 1671, Philip was pressured into signing a treaty making the Wampanoags subject to the laws and government of New Plymouth as well as subject to the king of England and forcing him to pay a fine and to pledge never to sell lands without Plymouth's approval. Quite obviously, Philip's resentment and hatred toward Plymouth continued to mount.

On the gender matter, women among southern New England Indians played important roles and did not confine themselves "wholly to drudgery in the field and by the fire." Women in the Wampanoag and some other neighboring Indian societies, however, seem to have performed more vital functions. The Wampanoag society was essentially matrilineal, although the patrilineal system was recognized, with definite divisions of labor and work between men and women.

Men usually performed the work that required heavy, physical labor, such as hunting, fishing, clearing land for planting by felling trees and removing stumps, constructing dugout canoes, and manufacturing and maintaining weapons and various implements. Hunting and fishing, which were both demanding and dangerous, were not play but work. Since these activities demanded "many hours of intense labor under hard conditions," the hunters and fishermen are said to have been in need of a "long period of recuperation."

Women, on the other hand, were responsible for raising and caring for children, gathering, making clothing, weaving, cooking, and serving meals. It has been argued that one of the major factors contributing to southern New England Indian women's being confined to a separate, domestic (private) sphere is the fact that "many women cannot, during substantial portions of their lives, perform tasks incompatible with child rearing." The notion of "separate spheres" of work for men and women, however, did not make one group's work superior or inferior to the other's, nor did it lead to unequal status in society for men and women.

Even the office of sachem in southern New England sometimes came to be held by women, including Weetamoo (Pocassets), Quaiapen (Narragansetts), Weunquesh (Eastern Niantics), and Awashonks (Sakonnets), to whom Philip sent six men in June 1675 to urge her to join him in opposing the English. Although the sachemship was usually passed on patrilineally, the daughters of sachems who died without male heirs occasionally succeeded to the office. The rule of hereditary succession was not strictly observed, and it has been pointed out that not only "the hereditary right" but "personal qualities" of candidates, both men and women, were important factors in selecting sachems. Thus "less able direct heirs" were sometimes rejected in favor of "more capable relatives."

During Philip's period, however, the English influence, especially accumulation of capital in the form of wampum and other goods, began to facilitate a patrilineal system, which in turn led to the decline of women's status, including that of woman sachems, in the Wampanoag tribes.

Christianity was another factor that caused a devastating effect on Indian society. To the New England Indians conversion did not mean merely believing in the Christian God and learning and accepting the Christian teachings. It went beyond religion, and the Indians were required to live in English-style settlements, wear English clothing, learn and speak English, and take on the entire English culture and civilization. Indians, in short, were forced to change their world in order to be Christians.

Philip always feared that the conversion of sachems would possibly mean the loss of his village and his whole group to the English world, thus reducing the source of tribute for him. Christianity also contributed to weakening the authority of the sachem, making him "a common man" among his people. It also discouraged converts from following traditional customs, including the payment of tribute to the sachem. Polygamy, which was most common among sachems, whose first wives were of high status (Philip had at least two wives), also came to be challenged as unclean. In addition, those Indians who rejected Christianity, as most of them did, would certainly reject the authority of a Christian sachem.

"If I become a praying sachem," Philip once remarked, "I shall be a poor and weak one, and easily be trod upon by others . . . and I shall be a great loser by praying to God." The religious leaders, powwows, who had formerly been well respected and much honored, were now ignored. They had always resented Eliot's preaching and became disturbed that the people would give up their own religion. ("Powwows" also referred to religious ceremonies; these eventually turned with the passage of time into something having little to do with religion, such as fairs, festivals, dances, athletic activities, and other gatherings.) Religious differences soon took a political form. During King Philip's War, the Wampanoags were divided, with some groups, like the Martha's Vineyard Christian Indians, supporting the English.

In Indian-English relations, Philip had to face more serious challenges. In the view of the Plymouth leaders, Massasoit's sons,
Wamsutta and Metacom, although they expressed their desire to
continue the policy of friendship, became bolder and more independent. The 1660s was no longer a period of amicable relations
as established by Massasoit. Edward Winslow, Massasoit's closest
English friend, died in 1655, William Bradford three years later,
and Massasoit in 1660. Their respective successors never became
friends, and the new Plymouth leaders no longer paid as much
respect to the Wampanoag supreme sachems as their predecessors had to Massasoit.

In 1662, the Plymouth authorities sent a force of armed
troopers to bring the defiant Alexander back forcefully to Plymouth, where he was subjected to an aggressive interrogation,
after which he soon died. Five years later, when Plymouth heard
of a rumor that Philip was planning to help the French attack
New England, it immediately sent a troop of horses to bring him
back to Plymouth for questioning.

In September 1671, when Philip attended the arbitration
meeting held by the delegates of Massachusetts and Connecticut
and the Plymouth officials, Philip was treated like a criminal defendant, although the meeting was to mediate the conflicts between Plymouth and the Wampanoags. Philip might have well
remembered such English practices, especially of the treatment
the Narragansett sachems received in 1645, when they were persuaded to meet with the United Colonies commissioners but
were forced to sign an arbitrary treaty under military threat.

The Wampanoags had never been the subjects of the Plymouth colony until the Treaty of September 29, 1671, but they
were under constant pressure from Plymouth. For King Philip,
who fiercely believed that the Wampanoags were never under
Plymouth jurisdiction, the question was not whether the English
law was fair or not. Since Indians had lived for a long time without the benefit of English law, Philip was ready to reject it whenever it was contrary to Indian interests.

When the Plymouth colony in 1662 objected to Alexander's
practice of selling land to someone other than the colony, he was

furious. Whose business was it except the sachem involved? Later the same year, Philip agreed not to sell land to "strangers" (English settlers not acceptable to Plymouth), and six years later, he signed a similar agreement, promising to sell his land only to the colony. Although the policy was in part designed to prevent fraud and safeguard the Indians' interest against unscrupulous colonists, Philip believed such rules should be ignored if they would not fit his purpose.

For the Wampanoags, the Plymouth policy of protecting the Indians against fraud and exploitation in land sales was not the issue. The real issue was "the proximity of settlements," especially the kind of settlements the Plymouth government was establishing nearby. Philip's troubles with surrounding English settlements had repeatedly demonstrated that such settlers were very detrimental to Wampanoag villages, creating all kinds of grievances for Philip's people. The cattle of English settlers, which were allowed by law to roam freely, for example, wandered around, invaded Wampanoag villages, and destroyed their unfenced cornfields. Also, unscrupulous settlers were eager to sell the Indians liquor without license, causing serious drunkenness among the natives.

If the Indians sold land, that would inevitably lead to the establishment of English settlements, about which the Indians could do very little. Then what could the Indians do? They could make sure that those English settlements would be beneficial. Alexander and Philip were not so much concerned about the sale prices or fairness of the sales. Many individual settlers, to be sure, paid more than did government-appointed buyers, but Alexander and Philip's main concerns increasingly were about what kind of settlement would be created and what kind of settlers would be moving in.

Instead of selling land to the Plymouth government and being forced to accept the settlements created by government policy, which usually were hostile, Philip wanted to sell land directly to prospective settlers he liked, who would surely become good neighbors and create the kind of settlements which would coexist with the Wampanoag villages peacefully.

What he at least wanted was to perpetuate the Wampanoag country, sharing the frontier with the kind of English he preferred to live side by side with, or to create the Wampanoag nation with English friends living on its peripheries to protect and support the Wampanoags. In fact, Philip might have very well dreamed of creating a greater Wampanoag nation, in which many friendly English lived in the surrounding area as an integral part of its population. For this reason, controlling land sales, by selling the land directly to carefully selected colonists whom he would like as desirable neighbors, was critically important to him. But this was not the kind of policy the Plymouth authorities were likely to entertain.

The drastic reduction of Massasoit's territory was not a sudden event. Philip, who simply continued the policy set by his two predecessors, kept on selling and surrendering his land until 1672, when he began to feel the pressure of English communities upon the tribal hunting and fishing grounds as well as cornfields.

Although he was the one who sold the land to the settlers relentlessly, Philip must have realized that his country was increasingly smaller and that the English who settled on the land monopolized it without sharing any of the natural resources on it. What about the Indian rights to hunt, fish, cut firewood, and of course to own acreage for agricultural use? When Philip finally saw that he was not sharing his land with the English settlers but losing it to them completely and forever, he became determined to retain what little was left. He confessed to one of his English friends, "But Little remains of my ancestor's domain, I am resolved not to see the day when I have no country."

Philip also took a more formal step to curb this trend. In 1672, he complained to Governor Thomas Prence about the continuing sale of Indian lands to the colonists and requested that the governor "would give them no answer" if anyone (Indian or English) asked to purchase their land. Philip also reminded the governor of his promise made in the previous year that Plymouth would make no further grants of land belonging to the Sakonnets (a Wampanoag affiliate under squaw sachem Awashonks) for seven years.

Another problem for the Wampanoags was the restrictions imposed on trade to protect the colony interests. For example, Plymouth prohibited trade with the Wampanoags in arms, liquor, horses, and boats. Occasionally, exceptions were made. King Philip's request to purchase a horse in 1665 was officially denied because the Plymouth authorities feared that it might set a bad precedent. They, however, gave him one as a gift.

Philip is known to have had ability as a diplomat, especially his skill of playing one against another, whether they were colonies or Indians. After his accession to the sachemship, Philip followed the traditional Wampanoag policy of hostility toward the Narragansetts. In 1666, in order to undermine the power of Ninigret, an able sachem of the Eastern Niantics (a close affiliate of the Narragansetts), who was the main target of English suspicion, Philip dictated a letter to one of the English officials on Long Island, warning him that Ninigret was determined to continue exacting tribute from the Indians there.

In the following year, when Philip was required to answer to a rumor that he had agreed to help the French attack New England, he denied the rumor and blamed the Narragansett Indians for hiring one of his men to start the rumor to cause trouble between the English and himself.

Such a strategy did not always work. His attempt in 1671 to secure the support of Massachusetts by playing it against Plymouth disastrously failed because the aggressive Plymouth policy was quickly agreed upon not only by the Bay Colony but by Connecticut. Philip, however, optimistically hoped that the relations with Plymouth might improve.

Governor Prence died in 1672 and was succeeded by Josiah Winslow. Kinder and more moderate, Winslow was the son of Edward Winslow, himself a former governor, Bradford's chief lieutenant in dealing with the Indians, and most important, a close friend of Philip's father. Philip had great hope that the Plymouth-Wampanoag relations would improve under the new governor. But his optimism was shattered when Plymouth continued to carry out its hard policy toward the Wampanoags even more aggressively.

CHAPTER 4

The Clash of Legal Cultures

For the Pilgrims, the first order of business in the New World was to establish their own community, modeled after that of England. They were not trying to settle among the Indians, but to create their society on the land carved out of Indian country. In order to ensure that English law would prevail within their settlement, it was, therefore, necessary to secure legal immunity from the Indians surrounding them to make sure that Indian law would not encroach upon their society.

Among the European countries, the basic rule of law that had long been practiced was territoriality—all people, regardless of whether they were citizens or foreigners, are equally subject to the law of the country where they live. What the Pilgrims were trying to do in establishing legal immunity from the laws of the natives (extraterritoriality) was to deviate from the common European practice. This concept of extraterritoriality, an exception to the general rule of Europeans, then, was in essence based upon the prejudice of Europeans toward non-European peoples: that the Asians, the Africans, and the American aborigines were all primitive, backward, and inferior infidels, and thus their laws were barbaric and uncivilized.

When the Europeans came to live in the New World, surrounded by native people, they quickly decided that they should not be subjected to the barbaric laws of these primitive people but should have the privilege and protection of the laws of their own countries. Through the treaties they concluded with the Wampanoag chief sachem, Massasoit, and other sachems within a year of their landing, the Pilgrims were able to secure this privilege, inducing the Indians to recognize English legal jurisdiction, including jurisdiction over Indian perpetrators against English residents, within the English settlement and its vicinity.

The basic legal relations the Pilgrims established with the neighboring tribes had been maintained for more than twenty years as Massasoit renewed his treaty in 1639. But as time went on, more colonists came, their settlements multiplied, their territory expanded, and consequently the English and native communities came closer, forcing the colonists to study the law of the Wampanoags as more legal problems arose from increasing English-Indian contact.

Most of the Plymouth settlers, however, did not respect the New England Indian legal system, and continued to dismiss it as "barbarous" and irreconcilable with their own system, therefore, unworthy of consideration. The law ruling the Wampanoag society, which was "primitive," self-sufficient, and preliterate, with the practice of hunting, gathering, and rudimental farming, was to the settlers not an attractive source of law from which they could learn.

As they became more familiar with the law of their neighboring natives, the colonists came to realize that Indian law was not simple, crude, and unsophisticated, but rather, a complex and effective system. It was not the backwardness of native law, then, but the vast difference between English and New England Indian legal principles and systems and their hopeless incompatibilities that troubled the settlers the most and perpetuated the notion that the laws prevailing among these native people did not merit their attention.

How did the two legal cultures differ? In the view of the Wampanoag and other New England Indians, law and justice were a personal and clan matter and did not involve a third party or an impersonal public institution or "state." This system of justice, involving a person or his clan compensating or punishing another party for an injury or loss, was in sharp contrast to the English practice of dependence on an institutional system for conflict resolution. To the Indians, therefore, such English legal apparatus as statutes, courts, juries, jails, sheriffs, and constables were meaningless. In some cases of public nature, the Indians believed that humor and ridicule directed at an offender by his fellow tribesmen were sufficient to compel the desired behavior.

The Algonquian legal culture, which was based upon the principle of blood feud and clan responsibility, made no distinction between criminal and civil law, hence no distinction between the civil wrong and crime, which were both matters of clan against clan, not public matters. Retributive justice was the essence of their law, and legal problems had to be solved by two parties: the offending and aggrieved parties in terms of wrong and revenge. A wrong was remedied by a revenge sought normally by the kin of the aggrieved party, and, quite naturally, different wrongs, such as tort, breach of agreement, assault, adultery, murder, and theft, required different forms of retribution.

Although private and interested parties carried out the execution of retaliation, they were not free to do anything at all, but were bound by tribal custom and sanction. Thus before it put retaliation into execution, the aggrieved party carefully weighed and considered the details and limits of the retaliation, lest it should exceed the acceptable bounds. If the party violated the code and sought revenge beyond the proper limit of retaliation for the initial wrong, it would subject the offender to further sanction, in the form of counterretaliation.

The New England Indian law defined and punished fewer wrongs than European law did in the category under "crimes." There were no crimes of fornication or "unnatural vice," nor was there any heresy, as defined by European law. All sexual relations except the rare cases of rape were personal matters, outside the jurisdiction of sachems and council.

Marriage among the Algonquians was an agreement, but not a legally binding contract as in the European sense, and therefore could be broken anytime at will from either side. Such a system would allow individuals to form more than one relationship simultaneously, polygamy, but in fact their marriages were usually monogamous and lasting relationships. Only on rare occasions did "adultery" become the target of retaliation. The wronged party would beat the offender, sometimes to death, which could not be revenged. Among Indians, there were no such things as crimes without victims.

The difference between Indian law and English law was most

sharply revealed in their differing concepts of homicide. Since murder was not a public matter but was a problem to be settled between two clans under the Indian law, all members of both the murderer's clan and the victim's clan became involved in the death. If a member of one clan killed a member of another clan, the victim's clan had the right to retaliate or take revenge against the aggressor, which in turn imposed on the perpetrator's clan the obligation to be "indifferent" and to subject itself to the retaliation.

This law of blood (blood feud), however, would not produce "a cycle of endless retaliatory killings" because one satisfactory retaliation, if it was done properly and within the limit of the recognized bounds, would end the entire affair. It must be emphasized that the law of vengeance was intended to restore "balance and harmony," as existed before between the groups, not to produce perpetual strife between them. Nor was the Indian blood feud as practiced in New England a cold-blooded, stoic, rigid system, because there was a widespread custom among the Indian communities of mitigating the wrong by material compensation, specifically by the offending clan's payment of valuable goods to the victim's relatives.

What happened when a murder was the result of the sachem's action against one of his men for such conduct as treason, betrayal, and other public acts against the group or sachem? As long as a death sentence was rendered with consultation and consensus, such a killing was beyond a clan matter. If a killing was done without such group approval, however, it might be more likely treated as a murder, and thus would be revenged by the kinsmen of the condemned. Executions were sometimes conducted in secret, when it was feared that public execution would cause a disruption, unrest, or disorder. These secret executions, which were occasionally reported in the colonial records, were really assassinations. Was John Sassamon sentenced to death and executed, murdered, or assassinated in this manner?

If a murder took place between two clans belonging to different groups (bands), it would still be an interclan matter, but it would more frequently become an interband affair, if the sachems and councilors of both groups became involved. Justice between two groups cannot be well defined. If one band was wronged by a member of another, compensation could be demanded, but it would be up to the offending side to decide whether they would accept such a demand. Satisfaction could be achieved by taking the offender's life or by receiving a monetary payment to compensate for material or human loss. If satisfactory remedies were not made, the offended party could try forcibly to take in lives or goods the equivalent to what had been lost.

The law of England, as well as other European nations, on the other hand, defined murder as an offense against the state, not a private matter between two groups of people. In order to protect the public interest, the governments of the English colonies in North America had the power and the duty to apprehend, try, convict, and punish the murderer. Under English law, the offender's intention was a vitally important concern to the judges in ascertaining the nature of the conduct and assessing the offender's culpability. By contrast, Indian law did not consider the offender's intention important. It was only the conduct that mattered.

Another significant distinction between Indian and English laws was their differing jurisdictional concepts. The Indian legal system was based upon personality—the principle that the law of the country of the individuals involved rules. For the Indians it did not make much difference where the crimes or other legal actions took place. It was the law of the country of the persons involved that would control the affair. There were, however, many unsettled problems in intertribal disputes as to which law, perpetrator's or victim's, plaintiff's or defendant's, would rule. Diplomatic negotiations would settle most of the specifics of these problems, and intertribal disputes were relatively easy to handle because all the southern New England tribes belonged to the same general legal culture.

More serious were the disputes between the Indians and the colonists, who had a totally different jurisdictional principle from that of the Indians. Plymouth and other English colonies adhered to the basic European rule of territoriality, the principle that the law of the place of action rules, regardless of who might be involved in the affair, citizens or noncitizens. Thus, a murder of an Indian by a Dutch person, for example, would be handled and tried by the Plymouth court if the murder took place within its jurisdiction. But the Indians would consider that they had the right to revenge against the Dutch.

The different laws of homicide between the English and the Indians in southern New England did lead to very complicated situations when cases involved Indians and the English. The jurisdictional problem of who handled these cases, of course, became an extremely serious matter, because some of the conduct was criminal in one jurisdiction but less serious, or even acceptable, in the other.

Indians and English, adhering to two different systems of "personality" and "territoriality," could both claim jurisdiction for the same case. The Plymouth court, for example, could claim its jurisdiction over a murder case for the reason that it occurred within Plymouth, while the Wampanoags could also claim jurisdiction on the ground that the victim or the offender was one of its members. Regardless of legal justification and reasoning, however, the jurisdictional problem was dictated by the simple fact of who seized the offender. In the 1638 Peach case already cited, it was the English who had apprehended the murder suspects and placed them in their custody. Although the Narragansetts demanded the transfer of the offenders because the victim was one of them, and their law of revenge should be applied, Plymouth insisted on trying the case. In the end, the Narragansetts agreed with Plymouth and could only witness the trial and executions.

Among "criminal" acts of the Indians, the most prevalent was assault. According to the law of revenge, the injured party could attack the assailant and return a favor by inflicting equivalent injury on the initial attacker if the matter was not settled by material compensation. If, however, an Englishman were a victim of an Indian's assault, the colonial court would impose corporal punishment, in addition to compensatory damages. Thus the offender would receive different treatment depending upon who handled the case.

New England Indians did not impose criminality on such conduct as sexual activities, infanticide, and theft, although they were clearly criminal acts in the English colonies. In general, Indian law not only defined fewer "crimes" than the colonial law but also dealt with them in a drastically different manner. It appears, therefore, that the colonial legal system worked in many instances to the disadvantage of the Indians.

On the whole, the Indian judicial system was very effective, despite the absence of written law and of European-type judicial institutions. Indian law, though it was essentially a set of binding social customs, was as real and enforceable as any statute of the colonial government. Individual tribal members knew, through training and custom, what was expected of them. Its complexity and effectiveness notwithstanding, the Indian legal system was not appealing to the English settlers, who were on the threshold of modern scientific civilization.

When two diverse cultures meet, the clash of cultures can lead to various situations: amalgamation, assimilation, or respectable coexistence. Although the Indians of southern New England had a sufficiently developed civil society and land-use pattern to justify their claims to ultimate ownership and jurisdiction, cultural coexistence could not be maintained on a permanent basis; in fact, it did not last for long.

As long as the popular view that the Indian was little better than a roving barbarian without law, government, or religion remained strong, the Pilgrim and Puritan leaders, who did not have great respect for Indian culture, were understandably reluctant to share the administration of justice with them. Some colonists, such as Roger Williams, at times did attempt to establish a principle of justice based upon full coexistence with the Indians, but such an ideology was too radical to be turned into a durable policy.

The dominant attitudes among settlers, which were the result of their low estimation of Indian law and of their consequent failure to fully appreciate its operation, produced a policy of expansion of English law as a better alternative to Indian law. The clash of English and Indian legal cultures brought about a one-way transformation, from Indian to white, allowing no room for Indian law. In the process, not only were Indians increasingly placed under the jurisdiction of English law, but also the law operating within their community began to be eroded by the force of colonial law.

Many factors contributed to this continuous unilateral expansion of English law. Religion played an important role. The Pilgrims and Puritans, who wanted to live the godly life, were anxious to enforce good behavior in others, because "the true convert" seeks to destroy all sin. A zealous enforcement of morality in others, including the natives, was another way of proving to themselves that they might have faith and be the saved. New Englanders considered that they must not only create a godly society but bring the gospel to the heathen. Successful conversion of the Indians would demonstrate God's approval of the Puritan migration to the New World, but they made no compromise; the Indians must not be allowed to be autonomous neighbors or even partial carriers of aboriginal culture, but must forsake their theology, their language, their political and economic structures, and all other aspects of their way of life. It was not merely acculturation but a complete transformation of the Indians into white men.

Although the New Englanders ultimately failed in this endeavor, their experiment stimulated the extension of their law to the Indians; the law was used as a means to achieve the religious end, and its consequent expansion over the Indians became one of the very manifestations of the Puritans' effort to propagate their religion. The drastic decline of the Indian population throughout the colonial period also contributed to the monolithic growth of English law. The fur trade, which affected almost every aspect of Indian village life, seriously weakening village society internally, also provided the New Englanders with the opportunity to enlarge their jurisdiction, thus devastating Indian society from without.

Perhaps the most damaging effect of European civilization was felt on the structure of Indian government, which had worked well among the New England Indians. The political system not only was seriously affected by the contact but, more important, could formulate no effective and unified policy for coping with the English regarding the fur trade, diplomacy, land, and law.

All these forces—Puritanism, Indian population decline and un-controlled influx of English immigrants, the fur trade, and the corresponding weakening of the Indian government structure—helped make easy the English path of legal expansion, which in turn contributed to the further decline of the Indian political system. In regulating Indian-English legal relations, for example, the English often insisted that disagreements and crimes be disposed of in the European fashion. Consequently, the political prerogatives of the council of elders or the clans of the village came to be assumed by Europeans, which not only weakened the functions of the elders and the clans but contributed to the breakdown of the basic village and other governmental structures.

The Indians' type of governmental system proved unsatisfactory for dealing with a nation-state like England because the Indian government, whether village or confederation, was in no position to make clear, uniform policies. Lack of consistent policies on the fur trade led to the ruthless exploitation of natural resources. The native government inadvertently allowed the unchecked penetration of Western civilization into native society, which led to a radical change in the nature of Indian material culture. In order to withstand these outside pressures, an effective, centralized, unified government was needed—a system irreconcilable with traditional Indian government.

Under such circumstances, the New England Indian groups could not for long maintain equal footing with the Puritans in legal relations. Yet, the failure of the English legal system to meet Indian standards of retributive justice in interracial crimes frequently forced the Indians to continue to seek justice in their own fashion. The Indians also rejected the colonists' excuse for not protecting the Indians against English perpetrators, but Indians themselves were increasingly unable to maintain their traditional legal system effectively within their own community. Early English contact seriously modified Indian society, undermining its legal system and function. English influence also made some Indians less respectful of their own legal system, freeing them to challenge and defy the sachems' authority.

The clash of legal cultures in New England took a peculiar

one-way form, because the English settlers had no intention of learning from the Indians. No significant changes took place in the English legal tradition as a result of Indian-white relations. It soon became apparent that New England cultural imperialism was incompatible with the survival of Indian societies, and English law, while adjusting itself to the peculiar circumstances of the New World, eventually expanded into Indian country without being modified by Indian law. Indians were the ones who had to adjust themselves to a different law. This pressure for legal transformation was most strongly felt by those Indians who lived near the English settlement and had close and constant contact with the settlers.

Indians, as ethnocentric as the Europeans, undoubtedly deeply resented the imposition of English law and tried desperately to hold on to their own legal culture as long as possible. In replacing an established legal system without any corresponding solicitude for the rights and interests of their new "subjects," the English caused dissatisfaction, anxiety, and hostility among the natives.

The Indians not only had to adjust themselves to the workings of a new legal system but also had to make major substantive adjustments: from clan responsibility to individual responsibility, from private retaliation to resort to state authority, and from a system based on their cultural values to a new criminal law prohibiting conduct (such as sexual activities) that had no criminality at all in the Indian culture. It was within this unfamiliar and soon detested framework that native Americans were compelled to seek justice and protect their rights. The Sassamon case and King Philip's War, which it triggered, stand as crucial events in this devastating transition in Indian legal culture.

CHAPTER 5

A Man Across Two Worlds:
The Career of John Sassamon

John Sassamon (his name is written in various ways, all abbreviations of his own spelling, Wussausmon) was born in Punkapog (now Canton, Massachusetts) sometime after 1620. He was the son of a Wampanoag Indian who with his wife and family lived in Dorchester. Sassamon's parents were among the few survivors of the epidemic that swept the coastal region in 1616–1618, but they were not lucky enough to escape the 1633 smallpox epidemic and died with a number of other Indians.

Many of these Indian victims were converted to Christianity on their deathbeds and left their children with English families so that they were taught English, Christianity, and the European way of life. John Sassamon, who was in his early teens at the deaths of his parents, was no doubt one of those orphans brought up by English families. It may very well have been that Sassamon came to live in the home of a prominent Dorchester resident, Richard Callicott, and learned how to read and write from members of his family. John Eliot, who had been the minister of the nearby town of Roxbury since 1632 and visited Dorchester frequently, must have known Sassamon from his childhood and taught him. It is also probable that Sassamon attended an Indian School in Dorchester, in which Eliot took a deep interest by visiting regularly and personally teaching the pupils.

During the Pequot War, Sassamon, just old enough to be in military service, served with his master Richard Callicott under Captain John Underhill, serving not only as an interpreter but also as a soldier. According to Underhill, when Block Island Indians among the Pequots were spying on Sassamon, who was wearing English clothes and holding a gun, they asked him from some distance away, "what are you, an Indian or an English?" "Come hither," Sassamon replied, "and I will tell you." As soon as they were close enough to see for themselves, "hee pulls up his cocke and let fly at one of them, and without question was the death of him." After the war, on their way home, Callicott and Sassamon were briefly entertained at the Providence home of Roger Williams, who negotiated with Callicott for Pequot captives.

They returned to Dorchester with their own Indian captives: Callicott brought a Pequot "little squaw" and a Montauk Indian named Cockenoe for servants, while Sassamon came back with a young Pequot woman who may have later become his wife. She was probably that "Pequot maid" who was appointed by the Massachusetts governor Thomas Dudley to serve as an interpreter when the Narragansett sachem Miantonomo came to Boston to negotiate with the Bay Colony authorities. Miantonomo first objected to having her as the interpreter, but he finally conceded and "did speak with our committees and us by a Pequot maid who could speak English perfectly." In 1645, Sergeant Callicott and Sassamon are recorded to have been present at a treaty signing in Boston.

Sassamon must have also resumed his contact with John Eliot after the war. Eliot, who by then had become very interested in the Indian language, began to employ Indian linguists, including Sassamon, to teach him their language, while teaching them in exchange English and the Christian way of life. Eliot did not do the translation of the Bible and numerous other religious texts into the Massachusett language by himself, but heavily relied on Indian translators and interpreters.

In the early 1640s, John Eliot took notice of the linguistic abilities of Cockenoe, the servant of Richard Callicott, and engaged this "pregnant witted young man . . . who pretty well understood his own language, and hath a clear pronunciation" as teacher and interpreter. By 1646 Eliot mastered the Massachusett language enough to be able to preach sermons in the language. By the end of the decade, however, Cockenoe, who had been released from his servitude, left Eliot and returned to Long Island, where he began a long career as an interpreter between the Montauk Indians and the English. Eliot in his stead made Sassamon his chief assistant, and Sassamon throughout his life served Eliot well in his missionary activities.

In 1651, when Eliot established the first "praying town" in nearby Natick, Sassamon was involved in Eliot's project from the beginning and soon became its schoolmaster. In fact, Sassamon was one of Natick Indian School's two native schoolmasters, who were entrusted with teaching, under Eliot's guidance, their young countrymen to spell, to read, and to write. He thus was surely among the elite of Praying Indians and became one of Eliot's favorite students. In 1653, two years before a special Indian College was opened at Harvard, Sassamon attended Harvard College through an arrangement made by Eliot. He did not stay in Cambridge for long, however, and returned to Natick within a year, although he was briefly a classmate of many fortunate sons of Massachusetts Bay, including John Eliot Jr., Samuel Bradstreet, Thomas Shepard, and Increase Mather.

After his return from Harvard, Sassamon continued to serve as a schoolmaster in Natick, but he seems to have fallen from Eliot's favor by 1654, when he and two other Natick Indians not only became obnoxiously drunk themselves but forced liquor on the young son of a pious Natick resident. This incident occurred about ten days before the examination that Eliot had scheduled as part of his plan for the Natick Indians' full participation in the Puritan community. Because of his misconduct, Sassamon was replaced by another Indian as a participant in the examination. Eliot wrote, "But his Apostacy at this time was a great triall, and I did lay him by for that day of our Examination, I used another in his room." Sassamon seems to have remained in Natick until 1656, however.

For several years after that, Sassamon's exact whereabouts are unknown, but he probably left Natick and went to the Wampanoag country, where he became the secretary of and interpreter for the chiefs. Some historians have argued that Sassamon had switched sides and went to work for the enemy, but he simply went back to the Indian group from which his father came. At any rate, Sassamon might have served the Pokanoket chief sachem,

Massasoit, and then his eldest son, Wamsutta, who succeeded him in 1660. By then Sassamon had assumed an important role for the sachem, participating as a scribe and translator in such treaty negotiations as the one between the Wampanoags and Rhode Island. When Philip became the chief sachem after his brother's death two years later, Sassamon came to perform a more influential function as Philip's scribe, interpreter, secretary, and counselor. Sassamon's mastery of English, his familiarity with the white man's way of life, and his general knowledge of the colonial situation were valuable to his master, who could not read or write English.

During the most part of the 1660s, therefore, Sassamon's name appeared again and again as witness to Philip's oath of loyalty to the English and as interpreter in treaty negotiations and in land transactions. Sassamon took full advantage of his ability to speak, read, and write both English and Massachusett, which became increasingly indispensable to Philip, but Sassamon's aggressive manipulation of his role led eventually to a falling out between the chief and his secretary/advisor.

As Sassamon gained the confidence of King Philip and attained an influential position among the Wampanoags, Eliot became very anxious to convert King Philip and enlisted Sassamon's influence on Philip. In 1664, at the very time when Sassamon was already working closely with Philip as a scribe and witness to treaties, Eliot asked the commissioners of Plymouth Colony "to give incouragement to John Sassamon, who teacheth Philip and his men to read." Eliot claimed that Philip, "did this winter past, upon solicitations and means used, sent to me for books to learne to read, in order to praying unto God, wch I did send unto him, and prsents with all." Eliot believed that Sassamon was "a means to put life into the work." But neither Sassamon's work nor the books Eliot sent were successful in converting Philip to Christianity. When Eliot visited Philip and offered to pray for his salvation, the sachem angrily responded by tearing a button off Eliot's coat and saying "That he cared for his gospel, just as much as he cared for that button."

In 1671, Eliot made another attempt, by sending two Natick Indian missionaries, Anthony and William Nahauton, whom John

Sassamon was requested to join, to preach to the Wampanoags. Philip, however, remained unconverted. English missionaries like Eliot strongly believed that the conversion of sachems was crucial in their endeavors because sachems, who had a great influence upon their subjects, would make the Christianization of the rest of the Indians much easier, but Indian chiefs, such as Philip, Uncas, and others, were usually concerned about whether their conversion would diminish their authority as sachems.

Sassamon did not stay at Mount Hope with King Philip for long. By the late 1660s, he was back among the Natick Indians, probably because John Eliot persuaded him to return. The reasons for his leaving Philip are a matter of conjecture. Some historians maintain that Sassamon had been under the influence of John Eliot from the beginning and essentially had acted as a spy, and as his attempt failed because his missionary zeal infuriated Philip, Eliot recalled Sassamon back to Natick.

According to John Easton, a Rhode Island Quaker, who had served as attorney general and was deputy governor of the colony then, one specific incident precipitated the break between King Philip and Sassamon. When Philip asked Sassamon to write his will, Sassamon (who was reported to be "a bad man"), pretending that he was writing down exactly what Philip dictated, named himself heir to a large part of Philip's land. When asked to read the document aloud, he read as if he had written what Philip requested. Sassamon was forced to flee when Philip discovered what he had done. Historians have made much of this incident, but one must remember that Sassamon had married Philip's favorite niece, and it was Sassamon's position in the family that might have prompted Philip to ask him to draw up the will. What Sassmon was accused of having done might not be excusable, but the will involved the distribution of Philip's property among his relatives, including Sassamon's wife.

Other historians simply argue that Sassamon's aggressive posture with his bilingual ability led to a personal conflict between him and Philip. Sassamon certainly exploited his literacy skills to gain a position of intimacy with Philip and to acquire status and prestige within the Wampanoag community.

Nevertheless, it would seem that there was no serious open breach with his countrymen on account of his returning to Natick; he still preserved friendly relations with Philip and his people afterward and freely mingled among them.

Back among the Christian Indians in Natick, Sassamon made a public profession of religion, was baptized, and became one of the ministers there. He then settled at Nemasket (part of present-day Middleboro), in Plymouth colony, where he served as preacher to the Praying Indians under the chief Tuspaquin, who had married Massasoit's daughter and Philip's sister, Amie. Sassamon had married their daughter Assowetough, whom the English called Betty. Alexander, whom Sassamon served as scribe, granted him lands near Assawompsett Pond for his service in 1662, just before Alexander died, and in 1673, the old chief, Tuspaquin, who encouraged the teaching of the Gospel, gave a twenty-seven-acre plot of land upon which to settle at Assawompsett Neck to Sassamon. The same year, Sassamon deeded the land to his daughter Betty and her husband Felix, although the old chief had just allotted fifty-eight and a half acres in Assawompsett to Felix.

Sassamon's departure, though it caused no open falling out with Philip, deprived Philip of Sassamon's valuable service as a go-between, marking the beginning of a steady deterioration of the once friendly relations between Plymouth colony and the Wampanoags. By the late 1660s many of the Wamapanoags were undoubtedly experiencing the growing hostility among the English, who had settled near their villages, while rumors of conspiracies supposedly planned by Philip had persuaded the Plymouth authorities to monitor his activities closely.

In 1671, a war scare was avoided without any bloodshed. A peace treaty was signed at Taunton on April 10, but it forced King Philip not only to accept the jurisdiction of the Plymouth government over the Wampanoags and to bind them to obey the colonial law but also to pledge to surrender to the colonists "all my English Armes to be kept by them for their security, so long as they shall see reason."

Relations, however, soon soured again over the interpretations of a treaty provision. While Philip had assumed that only the guns he and his men had brought to Taunton were to be surrendered, Plymouth stuck to the literal interpretation of the provision and insisted that Philip turn in every single firearm the Wampanoags possessed.

When Plymouth was planning a military expedition to confiscate all the guns belonging to the Wampanoags, John Eliot intervened. In early August Eliot instructed the Natick Praying Indians to send Sassamon and two other former missionaries, Anthony and William, back to the Wampanoags. Though they had failed to persuade the Wampanoags to accept Christ, these Natick Indians were determined to avoid war. They believed that the best way to settle the dispute was to ask Massachusetts Bay to intervene and convince Governor Thomas Prence of Plymouth that arbitration was far superior to actual fighting. In fact, Eliot had even instructed Sassamon to invite Philip to Boston.

While on his mission to the Wampanoags, Sassamon witnessed King Philip entertaining some leaders of the Sakonnets and many other Indian chiefs, including some Narragansett sachems, in order to solicit their support, and he reported their presence to the English colonists. Although the Plymouth authorities were furious about Philip trying to mislead Massachusetts Bay about their conduct and believed that Philip had to be subdued by force, they made a small concession to Eliot's arbitration plan and decided to consider the advice of both Rhode Island and Massachusetts, although they insisted that they still reserved the right to go to war against Philip, even if the other two colonies disapproved of the use of arms.

Meanwhile, the Plymouth authorities sent messengers to Philip and ordered him to appear before them to explain himself, but the sachem, who had been angry with John Sassamon for his informing Plymouth of the Narragansetts' visit, refused to indicate to the messengers whether he would obey the summons. King Philip had been deliberately evasive about Plymouth's demand because Eliot, through Sassamon, had invited him to Boston to talk with the Bay's leaders. When he visited Boston, Philip talked not only with the Bay's leaders but also with John Winthrop Jr., Connecticut governor, who happened to be in the city. These colonial leaders subsequently wrote to Governor Prence, pointing out that no previous agreement had made the Wampanoags subject to Plymouth and demanding that the Plymouth governor accept arbitration by Massachusetts and Connecticut.

On September 24, 1671, the arbitrators met at Plymouth and were joined by Philip. By the time the representatives from Massachusetts and Connecticut heard the controversy between Plymouth and Philip, their attitudes toward the Wampanoag chief had suddenly and drastically changed. They were now convinced that Plymouth's treatment of Philip was just. Acting in full unison with Plymouth, the arbitrators decided that the sachem was totally at fault and ordered him "to amend his wayes." Philip, now facing the united foes from the three colonies, had no choice but to accept the arbitrary treaty, which was concluded on September 29.

He was forced to acknowledge himself subject to Plymouth and the king of England. This must have reminded him of the Narragansetts' confrontation with the Massachusetts authorities in 1644, when the Narragansett sachems submitted their act of submission in order to challenge the Bay Colony, demanding it to stay out of their problems. Although nothing came out of it because the king, in the middle of the Puritan Revolution, had no power to intervene, this could have taught Philip an important lesson. Since he was forced to be made a subject of the king of England, Philip could use the power of the king effectively to prevent Plymouth from ordering him around. Unfortunately, however, Philip did not have forceful advisors like Roger Williams and Samuel Gorton, who took the Narragansetts' problems seriously. (This situation has a parallel in American Indians' claiming treaties' superiority to state law in the nineteenth century.)

The treaty also prohibited him from selling land or going to war against another Indian group without the approval of the Plymouth governor, required him to kill five wolves a year, and ordered him to pay the colony one hundred pounds within three years. In addition, Philip agreed that in case of trouble between the Wampanoags and the settlers he would submit the matter to the colonial authorities. In November 1671, Philip's younger brother, Takamunna, who had just come of age, signed a similar agreement. The heavy fine imposed on Philip caused him deep resentment and anger, but nevertheless he did pay up. He sold twelve square miles to Taunton for one hundred forty-three pounds, this time without Plymouth's permission! After paying his fine of one hundred pounds, Philip still had plenty of cash left, which he used not only to replace the guns he was forced to surrender earlier at Taunton but to buy more gunpowder. The victory Plymouth enjoyed in 1671 was thus not all one-sided.

The situation remained calm on the surface until late 1674, although the loss of a large amount of land in July 1674 to a Rhode Islander, based upon a bond he secured from Alexander in 1661, increased the Wampanoags' concern over land.

In the fall of 1674, a month before John Sassamon died, King Philip sent him with six others of his council across Mount Hope Bay by canoe to persuade the Sakonnet squaw sachem Awashonks to support his impending plans against the English. She had an army of three hundred. Awashonks honored Philip's envoys by calling her people together "to make a great dance, which is the custom of that nation when they advise about momentous affairs." Sassamon and one of her own councilors, George, slipped down to Benjamin Church's farm to warn him of the plot. Church, taking with him "Charles Hazelton, his tenant's son" as his interpreter, followed them back to Awashonks's village, where he saw "Awashonks herself in a foaming sweat was leading the dance," but as soon as she saw Church, she "broke off, sat down, calls her nobles round her, orders Mr. Church to be invited into her presence." Church was finally able to secure a promise from Awashonks that she and her army would be neutral if war should come. Quite naturally, Philip was enraged at her defection.

At the end of 1674, when Philip and his men were on a hunting trip in the vicinity of Sassamon's town, Nemasket, Sassamon went to the campsite. It is not known exactly why he went. Perhaps Sassamon still hoped that the Wampanoag sachem might be converted. Or Philip might have summoned Sassamon so that he could reprimand the Indian minister for betraying him by informing the Plymouth authorities of his entertaining the Narragansett visitors three years earlier and for failing his recent mission to Awashonks. Or Philip, who was rumored to have been soliciting many Indian groups to join him in his plans for the extermination of the English settlers, might even have invited Sassamon to enlist his advice on some matters or, more specifically, to persuade him to help recruit the Praying Indians in support of Philip's challenge against the English. Arguments over some important matters must have transpired between them. They might have violently disagreed and quarreled. One can only speculate. In the course of the discussion, Sassamon may have been convinced that Philip was indeed contriving a scheme to attack the English settlers and drive them away from the country. The meeting apparently broke up abruptly, and Sassamon left right away for Plymouth.

Sassamon met Governor Josiah Winslow of Plymouth at his house, "Careswell," in Marshfield and revealed Philip's plan to attack the English and expressed fear for his life. He confessed to the governor his fear that if Philip should know of his betrayal, that is, his revealing the plan to the Plymouth authority, Philip would immediately order him to be killed. But Sassamon failed to convince Winslow, because the governor had recently received so many similar warnings from other Christian Indians that he thought none of them should merit serious consideration.

Frustrated, Sassamon left Plymouth for home, but did not arrive at his town. Later, his body was found in Assawompsett Pond, a few miles south of his home town and near the land he had recently deeded to his daughter and her husband. Instead of returning directly to his town, Sassamon, who had feared for his life, might have been hiding himself in his family estate from Philip and his men, who now understandably considered him a traitor. He seemed to have been ice fishing upon the nearby lake and might very well have accidentally fallen into the water. Strong suspicion of foul play led eventually to a full investigation by Plymouth authority. Although the formal examination proved that Sassamon was not drowned, it was not conclusively proven that he was murdered.

Sassamon was, according to one contemporary, "one of the brightest and ablest praying Indians," who became well Christianized, anglicized, and literate, but he still retained some degree of Indianness within him, though living in a society modeled after the English community. More than once, his deviant behavior disappointed Eliot. He was also keenly aware of the importance of his rare bilingual ability and aggressively exploited it in Wampanoag society. Moreover, he does not seem to have had the most agreeable, congenial personality, as attested by some contemporary colonists. William Hubbard, for example, portrayed him as "a very cunning and plausible Indian, well skilled in the English language."

What kind of English did Sassamon write? King Philip's letter to Governor Prence written by him in the early 1670s reads:

KING PHILIP desire to let you understand that he could not come to the Court, for Tom his interpreter has a pain in his back, that he could not travil so far, and Philip sister is very sick. Philip would entreat that favor of you and aney of the majestrates, if aney English or Enjians speak about aney land, he pray you to give them no answer at all. This last somer he made that promis with you, that he would sell no land in 7 yers time, for he would have no English trouble him before that time. He has not forgot that you promis him. He will come as sune as possible he can speak with you, and so I rest
Your verey loveing friend
Philip, dwelling at mount hope nek.

Taking advantage of his ability, which few Wampanoags had, he tried to enhance his position and status and to promote even his selfish, personal interests.

By so doing, he must have caused deep resentment among many Wampanoags, especially jealousy from some of the tribal leaders, as he won a growing confidence from Philip. To many Pokanokets, Sassamon must have come to be seen as aggressive, dangerous, untrustworthy, wicked, and un-Indian. Sassamon's effective exploitation of his linguistic ability to promote his position and interest might have also led to his personality clash with his master, Philip.

John Eliot, who had known Sassamon from childhood on for more than forty years, noted Sassamon's death in his diary with sorrow, praising him simply as "a man of eminent parts & wit."

CHAPTER 6

Sassamon Found Dead

When the group of local Indians found John Sassamon dead in water under ice, they pulled the body from the water, took it to the shore of the frozen pond, buried it there, and went on their own way. It is not clear in the records whether they recognized the dead person as the minister of the Indian praying village, Nemasket, which became part of Middleborough (the present town of Middleboro), when it was incorporated in 1669.

They probably were not much concerned about who he was and how he died: whether murdered, killed accidentally, or a suicide. Such matters may not have been serious worries for the Algonquians unless a dead person was somehow related to them or was a close acquaintance. They did the best thing indifferent persons could do when they encountered a dead body.

When William Nahauton, another Praying Indian and Sassamon's close friend, realized that the dead man was the missing Sassamon, he reported the incident to the Plymouth authorities; they immediately became suspicious of foul play and decided to investigate the cause of death. Just less than a month earlier Sassamon had gone to see Governor Winslow to warn him of Philip's plans to make war against the colony and had expressed fear for his life, pleading with the governor for protection. Now the Plymouth governor, who had not paid much attention to Sassamon's warning at that time, immediately empowered the Middleborough constable to investigate the case and to appoint a jury of inquest (coroner's inquest) to ascertain the cause of the death. The records do not reveal any information on whom the constable, Jabez Howland, impaneled on the coroner's inquest or whether any of the twelve impaneled members was an Indian.

The constable and the jury of inquest exhumed Sassamon's body and subjected it to a careful examination.

The Plymouth colony, as early as the 1630s, had established the practice of appointing a jury of inquest to hold an inquiry whenever a person died unexpectedly or under suspicious circumstances or was simply found dead. The usual procedure was an actual investigation by a coroner (or a constable where no coroner resided), appointment of a jury of inquest by the coroner, and the jury decision "after a view of the body." Not only the settlers but all Indians within the jurisdiction of the Plymouth colony who came to an untimely death were thus passed upon by the jury of inquest in the same manner.

This practice of having the coroner investigate the cause of death originated in England in the tenth century and had become a well-established investigatory system in England by the early seventeenth century, when it was transplanted to North America by the English settlers. The well-developed, efficient investigatory system of the English coroner's jury, however, did not routinely rely on expert opinions of medical doctors to determine the causes of untimely deaths until the eighteenth century because until then doctors' opinions were considered not so reliable.

It was in Continental Europe that forensic medicine had first been developed. The French, beginning in the early eleventh century, had increasingly used surgeons as experts in courts. In Italy, the Popes' legislation, as reflected in canon law, greatly contributed to the growth in legal medicine, stipulating that medical experts should determine the character of the wounds. By the beginning of the fourteenth century, the medicolegal postmortem came to be practiced in Bologna. Soon many other Italian cities, such as Padua, Genoa, Florence, and Milan—which also played influential roles in the formation of modern economics, political thought, and the arts—followed suit and contributed to the establishment of modern legal medicine.

In Germany, medicolegal science received its first strong legal foundation in the laws of J. von Schwarzenberg and of the German Holy Roman Emperor Charles V in the early sixteenth century. These laws required not only "serious examination and, if necessary, opening of the body" in the case of violent death but also the use of medical experts in cases of infanticide, abortion, or medical malpractice. Thus in some German states, though not so advanced as in France and Italy, the legal foundation for the development of forensic medicine as a special scientific discipline had already been laid in the late sixteenth and early seventeenth centuries.

The slowness of the English in developing forensic medicine was partly due to the effective operation of the coroner system, even though it required lay, nonmedical officials to deal with medicolegal problems. It was not until the Continental European forensic medicine advanced so much that it began to surpass the English system that the English began to incorporate legal medicine into their system.

Although modern forensic medicine was not fully developed and practiced in the United States until the early nineteenth century, general knowledge of the medicolegal science prevailing in Europe and England came to be known in the English colonies in the seventeenth century. As early as 1647, the General Court of Massachusetts Bay colony authorized a postmortem for the purpose of teaching medical students. It was indicated that "an autopsy should be made on the body of a criminal once in four years."

An autopsy was also performed in 1663 in Guilford, Connecticut, by a medical doctor. When Elizabeth Kellin, the eight-year-old daughter of John Kellin, died unexpectedly, the suspicion of witchcraft arose. The Connecticut General Assembly authorized Dr. Bryan Rosseter to perform a postmortem examination on her and voted to pay him twenty pounds. After the autopsy, Rosseter ruled that the girl's death was caused by preternatural forces. The same year Rosseter performed another autopsy, at the request of the decedent's family, on the body of the Reverend Samuel Stone, who had died suddenly. The early colonial physicians thus started to dissect dead bodies not only to gain knowledge of anatomy but to ascertain the characteristics of the disease process and the cause of death.

The last four decades of the seventeenth century were a critical, transitional period in the development of forensic medicine in America. At the beginning of the period, the postmortem examination, though starting to be utilized, was performed in a sporadic and informal manner. Nor were there many medical doctors specializing in the field. By 1691, when Dr. Johannes Kerfbyle and five other physicians performed an autopsy ordered by New York's Provincial Council on the body of its newly elected governor Henry Sloughter, whose death had been suspected as being by poison, and ruled that a defect of his blood and lungs, not poisoning, was the cause of death, the practice was becoming more public and regular. By then, more specialists were also available, and the settlers seem to have recognized the importance of forensic pathology in the investigation of unnatural deaths.

But in the 1670s, when John Sassamon died mysteriously, the postmortem examination was far from being accepted as routine practice. Those physicians who had been trained enough or were experienced enough to perform such an autopsy were still few in number in the colonies. The autopsy was not fully accepted as general practice. The services of the doctors who specialized in autopsy were available, however, within a reasonable distance. The coroners' juries, therefore, could easily secure expert opinions of surgeons and physicians, if necessary, although they did not yet routinely solicit such opinions. The constable and inquest jury in Middleborough, however, decided to rely on their own judgment, based only upon external evidence and circumstances, to determine the cause of Sassamon's death.

The first duty for the investigating officers who would examine the external condition and appearance of the body was to view the body exactly in the position in which it was found. Such a rule had been recognized by Plymouth colony, which passed a law that if a person died unexpectedly, burial was specifically prohibited, upon the penalty of five pounds, before the coroner (or the constable) was informed of the death. For John Sassamon it was too late. His body had already been pulled from the icy water, taken to the shore, and buried. Those Indians who discovered Sassamon's body not only were unfamiliar with such laws but also were unaware of the necessity of investigating the deaths of persons who died unnaturally. The Plymouth investigating officers were thus faced with the difficulty of determining the cause of death by examining the disinterred body of Sassamon, who had been dead for at least two weeks.

During the entire period of Plymouth history, the *Plymouth Colonial Records* reported fifty-eight cases of untimely deaths, including two Indian deaths, that the coroners and juries of inquest were empowered to investigate. Strangely enough, the investigation of Sassamon's death by an inquest jury was not officially recorded. Except for a brief description made by the Reverend Increase Mather of Boston, who attended the inquest jury's investigation, nothing is available on the kind of inquiry the coroner's inquest made. Was the exclusion by oversight or intention? Nor do other accounts kept by contemporaries, all of whom were English colonists, provide any detailed information on Sassamon's death. Moreover, these personal accounts often contradict one another. Such meager and conflicting evidence in the records makes it extremely difficult to find out what exactly happened to Sassamon.

Lack of detailed accounts in the records could mean either that a detailed investigation, though actually performed, simply went unrecorded or that no extensive examination was ever conducted. All the information we can muster on the case is that the Middleborough constable and the jury of inquest, after hearing the report that no water had come out of the stomach and noticing some suspicious injuries (the extremely swollen head, the broken neck, and several other wounds on his body), concluded that Sassamon was not drowned but was thrown into the water after he was killed. Were these external signs the inquest jury examined conclusive enough to arrive at the determination that Sassamon was indeed murdered and then thrown into the water?

It may very well be that the Plymouth investigators examined the death thoroughly and came to an indisputable conclusion, but there is no hard evidence to prove that any careful examination ever was conducted. Or did they decide to limit themselves to only a few superficial tests? Such questions as to specifically how Sassamon's death was investigated, how the jury of inquest arrived at its decision, whether the inquest jury came to its conclusion with certainty or based upon meager and precarious evidence, remain unanswered.

The Indians who discovered Sassamon's body in the water under the ice found on the ice his hat and gun and a brace of ducks, but nothing else. No mention is made of the clothes he was wearing. Was there any blood on the ice? Who broke the hole in the ice upon the pond, through which Sassamon's body was supposed to have been slipped? What was Sassamon doing at the pond? Was he on his way back from his hunting trip? Or was he ice fishing? All he needed for fishing through a hole in the ice of the pond was a line. Weren't Sassamon's relatives living in the area summoned to testify and fill in the missing parts of the story?

If a person was found dead in water, the first thing the coroner and the inquest jury had to decide was whether the person actually drowned or was killed and then thrown into the water. If drowned, it was necessary for them to make a more difficult decision: whether the drowning was the effect of natural causes, accident, suicide, or homicide (thrown into the water when alive).

The rules to test whether a person drowned commonly prevailing throughout Europe in the seventeenth century had been established by a French medicolegal specialist, Ambroise Paré. He argued that the body of a person who had been drowned or thrown into the water while living had three main characteristics:

(1) the stomach and intestinal canal were filled with water
(2) a glaring mucus issues and sometimes a bleeding from the nose
(3) a frothy appearance about the mouth and the excoriated condition of the extremities of the fingers as if, in dying, the person had grasped the sand, or some other hard substance.

The seventeenth-century scholars of forensic medicine generally agreed that these three characteristics should not be considered independently as essential marks of death by drowning because there were so many exceptions to the rules. No single proof taken separately was considered perfectly satisfactory, and all three must be considered together in order to arrive at a just conclusion. These rules were familiar in general terms to colonial lawyers, doctors, and coroners, but it is uncertain whether the knowledge was widespread enough to be accepted by the local officials in towns like Middleborough.

The Indians who first found Sassamon's body testified that no water came out of the mouth when they pulled the body out of the pond. Could their statement be taken at face value? These Indians, who would not have been aware of the importance of water coming out of the drowned person's mouth, might have paid little attention to any water that did come out. Moreover, the Indians might have carried Sassamon's body downward, causing the water to drain away without their noticing it.

Even though the fact should definitely be established that Sassamon's stomach was not filled with water, such a finding would not rule out the possibility of his having been drowned. Although the presence of water in the stomach is in most cases an indication of the person's drowning, water in the stomach is an accidental circumstance, and in no way connected with the cause of death. During the struggles of a drowning person, a quantity of water might be swallowed, but in some cases a person might swallow little water. In order to show the full significance of water in the stomach of someone who may have drowned, it is necessary to prove that the water was neither swallowed before death nor injected after death.

Nor do the records show whether the jury of inquest investigated other marks for death by drowning such as a glaring mucus and a bleeding from the nose, a frothy appearance about the mouth, and the excoriation of the fingers. If drowning could not be ruled out as a possible cause of Sassamon's death, it is necessary to explore various forms in which death could have taken place when Sassamon was drowned.

What was the disposition of Sassamon's mind when he died? About a month earlier, Sassamon had met with King Philip, who was then visiting his hunting grounds near Sassamon's town, Nemasket, and the meeting seems to have broken up with serious disagreement between them. Sassamon then traveled to Marshfield to see Governor Winslow, warned him of Philip's impending conspiracy plans against the English, and expressed his fear that if Philip should know that Sassamon had betrayed him by revealing Philip's plans to the Plymouth authorities, Philip would immediately order him to be killed.

Winslow, however, did not take Sassamon's warning seriously nor attempt to protect his life, although the governor belatedly decided with the advice of his council to send his delegate to Philip to inquire of the truth of the matter. Sassamon must have felt angry and suffered deep disappointment and hopelessness. Instead of returning to his town, he seems to have been hiding himself in the wooded land he owned near Assawompsett Pond. Under such circumstances, Sassamon could have died in any possible situation.

Was there any possibility for Sassamon to die a natural or accidental death? Sassamon, who was in his mid-fifties, could have had a heart attack or stroke and fallen into the water. Was the ice-fishing hole large enough for a person to fall through easily? Was he drinking heavily? Since intemperance predisposes to stroke (sanguineous apoplexy), Sassamon, if he was drinking, could have had apoplexy and then slipped into the icy water. The records say that Sassamon's head was swollen, and the swollen head is regarded as one of the two most common signs of death from apoplexy. Or perhaps he was drunk and fell on the ice, slipped into the water, and had a heart attack and then died. If Sassamon fell into the water during a state of intoxication and never made an effort to save himself, or conversely, if Sassamon was in a state of syncope when drowned, not much water would have been swallowed nor would any dirt or sand be found under the nails.

Or was there any possibility of his having merely accidentally fallen into the pond through the hole and drowned, while the sharp ice hurt his head and neck and other parts of his body? Can one assume with certainty that Sassamon did not make an attempt on his own life? Sassamon might have thrown himself into the water and struck the hard ice, and the body might have thus been wounded. Considering Sassamon's depressed state of mind, the suicide theory cannot be completely ruled out, although suicide was not prevalent among the Algonquians. Moreover, he was a Christian and would have known what suicide might bring. To decide whether death is the result of suicide or homicide has always been one of the most difficult questions in medicolegal cases, especially in cases like that of Sassamon, who was found dead in water and whose body was not examined for a long time.

If Sassamon was either murdered by being thrown into the water while alive or drowned, instead of being murdered and then thrown into the water, his body must have had distinct external marks, some of which, it must be emphasized, would have been similar to those noticed by the Middleborough officials when they examined Sassamon's body.

On viewing Sassamon's head, the inquest jury simply noted that it was "extreamly swollen." There is no indication that a careful inspection was made to examine all possible injuries, including the strength of the bones and the fracture on the skull. No "violent blows to the head" have ever been recorded in any source, and the investigators seem to have failed to examine the body minutely enough that they could with certainty ascertain whether there were any wounds, bruises, or fractures capable of inducing death.

The swollen head noted by the inquest jury is one of the characteristics of a person drowned or found dead in water, but it does not seem to have been the result of any fatal wounds, bruises, contusions, fractures, or luxation. The swollen head is also one of the most common signs of death from apoplexy. The only sure way to find out is to dissect the head to find out whether there was a hemorrhage.

Moreover, the swelling of the head often indicates an incipient putrefaction of the body. When the Indians pulled Sassamon's body out of the water, it was the end of January, and the weather must have been very cold. The body, therefore, might have been in the water without seriously becoming putrid, but the process of putrefaction must have definitely started.

The broken neck was another condition of Sassamon's body noted by the jury of inquest. Increase Mather, who had attended the inspection conducted by the coroner's inquest, stated that Sassamon's neck was broken by the "twisting of his head around; which is the way that the Indians some times use when they practice murthers." Does this mean that the inquest jury was convinced that Sassamon died of a broken neck?

Killing a person by twisting the neck around was in fact also known as a mode of homicide in Europe in the sixteenth and seventeenth centuries. Since it would require a person to use strong force and violence to kill an individual in this way, this means was not very commonly used. (However, it would be easier to cause such damage if the person was dead already.) This mode of killing, therefore, seems to have been the least likely method a killer might have used. Why would the Wampanoag suspects, or anyone else, resort to such a strenuous method while many other easy options were readily available, unless the killer was extremely strong?

Murdering a person with the use of force would cause the victim terror, which would be manifested externally by a much suffused face, bloodshot eyes, redness of the visage, and terrified facial expression. Did those who examined the body see any of this, or did they only recognize the pale countenance, the livid and swollen face?

Was there any possibility of the Indians breaking Sassamon's neck by handling the body roughly and carelessly (frequently turning and bending the head) when they took it to the lake shore?

The inquest jury did not recognize any sign of strangulation in the Sassamon case. If a person has been strangled to death, a horizontal discolored circle is observed around the neck, and such discolorations are a very distinct red color and pass all around the neck. But if a person is strangled after death, these spots on the neck are of a livid color, distinguishable from contusions on the living body. The silence in the available records about such marks on the neck suggests several possibilities: the inquest jurors closely examined Sassamon's neck and found some marks but felt no need to make a note of it, they found no noticeable marks, or they simply neglected their duty to examine the neck properly.

Wounds received before and after death have distinct characteristics. Did the coroner's inquest make a minute inspection to look into such unusual marks? While wounds such as contusions and blows received before death are marked by red, bloody, and separated edges, those inflicted afterward are livid, and their edges close to each other, no inquiry seems to have been made on such a distinction. What kind of wounds were the several wounds on Sassamon's body the investigators recognized, and how were these bodily harms inflicted? Was he hit or struck by some object? Were the marks of wounds the result of accident attending submersion, the result of the drowning person's desperate attempt to grasp anything, including sharp ice? Were these bodily wounds fatal? Again, only a dissection could provide an answer.

When a person is thrown into the water, whether dead or alive, the body will sink. As the process of putrefaction begins, producing gaseous matters that make the body lighter than water, the body will rise to the surface. When the Indians found it first, Sassamon's body was floating on the water under the ice. This means the body had already started to putrefy, though the process had not yet advanced to any significant stage.

A human body (or an animal body) lying under water eventually becomes converted into a fatty substance called adipocere. Under normal circumstances, it takes a month in water for the body to form a small quantity of the fatty substance, and five or six weeks to produce a large quantity. Considering the fact that Sassamon's body was found in the water under the ice in late January, the New England winter must have delayed the progress of putrefaction and prevented any such substance developing in Sassamon's body.

In the water, the integument of the legs becomes indigo color, which turns brownish when exposed to the air, while the rest of the body is very white, which is converted into brown and green when taken out of the water. If the body remains very long in the water, abrasions of a bluish-brown tinge develop on the skin, indicating the commencement of putrefaction. This condition of the skin, which has the appearance of wounds being inflicted, could be mistaken for wounds and bruises.

{ *Igniting King Philip's War* }

To make matters worse, in incipient putrefaction, a rough treatment of or little violence on the body might cause rupture of the cutaneous blood vessels, causing an effusion of blood under the skin and a consequent ecchymosis. Sassamon's body had been removed from the water, buried, and then disinterred for the purpose of inspection, after at least one week of burial. The several wounds the inquest jury recognized on Sassamon's body could have been merely marks indicating that putrefaction was already under way. They might also have been minor injuries and probably not so visible when the body was first taken out of the water, but the gradual process of putrefaction might have developed these injured parts into conspicuous spots. Or were these indeed wounds showing major injuries?

This analysis seems to lead to a strong impression that the Middleborough inquest jury's finding was inconclusive and that there were no decisive proofs of assassination. Despite the meager evidence, the inquest jury did not seek expert medical opinion. Why didn't the Plymouth authorities consider the suspected murder of John Sassamon, though the victim was an Indian, serious enough to merit an autopsy on the body? The Guilford, Connecticut, doctor, Bryan Rosseter, who had already performed two autopsies a dozen years earlier, or some other specialist from the closer Boston area, could easily have been invited to perform a postmortem on Sassamon's body. More importantly, weren't the Middleborough constable and coroner's jury strongly affected by the general sentiment and feeling against the Wamoanoags among the Plymouth colonists, especially those living in the frontier towns? They may have felt no need to investigate the death thoroughly because they wanted to use the case merely to force Philip to conform. They may have predetermined that Philip and his Wampanoags were guilty and been convinced that they had sufficient evidence to prove murder against the Wampanoags.

As if to reassert their conviction, when Tobias, one of Philip's own counselors, was brought to review the body of Sassamon, it started "a bleeding afresh, as if it had newly been slain," although he had been dead and buried "for a considerable while before." This test, called "cruentation," a confrontation based on the belief that the corpse of the victim would start bleeding again at the approach of the murderer, was one of the supernaturalistic "tests" (including the ordeals by fire and water) prevailing among the Germanic barbarians who overran the Roman Empire. It was passed down well into the seventeenth century, and eventually was transplanted to the English colonies in North America as a method to prove the guilt of the accused.

Although it had never been a rational way to ascertain the guilt of the accused, the phenomenon proves to have been not completely a supernatural occurrence. On the commencement of putrefaction, the epidermis gradually separates from the skin, and a large quantity of blood extravasates and pools in between, making an appearance of contusions (ecchymoses), which can be easily interpreted as the result of a blow inflicted. When the skin breaks, the blood comes out. This phenomenon occurs particularly in those who die suddenly and full of blood.

The evidence was so far inconclusive, but three Wampanoag men, Tobias, Wampapaquan (son of Tobias), and Mattashunnamo, though they persistently denied their guilt, were arrested. Then an Indian by the name of Patuckson came forward, claiming to have seen these three Wampanoags commit the murder and throw Sassamon's body into the water through a hole in the ice in order to conceal their crime. Accordingly, on March 1, 1675, the three Wampanoag prisoners were formally indicted for the crime. The bill of indictment reads:

> Att this Court three natives were araigned, vizs, Tobias, & Wampapaum, and Mattushannama, for that being acused, that they did with joynt consent, upon the 29 of January, anno 1674, att a place called Assowamsett Pond, wilfully and of sett purpose, and of mallice fore thought, and by force and armes, murder John Sassamon, an other Indian, by laying violent hands on him and striking him, or twisting his necke, until he was dead; and to hide and conceale this theire said murder, att

the time and place aforsaid, did cast his dead body through a hole of the iyce into the said pond.

Meanwhile, Philip visited Plymouth on his own and voluntarily testified before the General Court that he had no role in the death of John Sassamon. Although the Plymouth leaders were not fully convinced of his innocence, they had no choice but to allow Philip to return home because they had no tangible proof to implicate him.

CHAPTER 7

Legal Imperialism:
The Murder Trial and the Executions

The Plymouth authorities, in full consultation with the Massachusetts leaders, decided that the Plymouth court should hear the case because the murder of Sassamon took place within the jurisdiction of Plymouth colony, although all involved in the case were Indians. This was in accordance with the English rule of territoriality, by which the law of the land where a crime is committed rules, quite contrary to the Indian legal system, based upon kinship and consanguinity, in which the law of the land of the individual parties rules.

No earnest effort was made on the part of Plymouth to negotiate with the Wampanoag sachem on jurisdictional matters. Some plans for impartial arbitration of this conflict between the Plymouth colony and the Wampanoag tribe, to be sure, had been suggested. Philip was willing to negotiate, but Plymouth flatly rejected the proposals; Plymouth magistrates were adamant enough to nip any possibility for such talks.

The case was heard before the General Court at Plymouth, which was not only a legislature but also a judicial body. Since its establishment in 1621, the General Court annually had elected a governor and assistants as the main body of the colonial government. Gradually, however, the Court of Assistants, which consisted of the governor and seven assistants, lost its legislative function, and eventually in 1646, the General Court ordered the governor and assistants, when they sat as the Court of Assistants, to limit themselves to judicial concerns, thus making itself the sole governing authority in the colony.

Earlier, the General Court had met four times a year—in March, June, October, and December—but in 1645, the December session was omitted. Until 1642, the Court of Election, as part of the General Court, was held in March, but thereafter the time was changed to June, because so many freemen, who by then lived far away from the town of Plymouth, had to come to Plymouth "tramping through the late snow and ice of March" to attend the election court.

Although the Court of Assistants was the principal court of justice, the General Court served as a judicial body in addition to functioning as a legislature. They therefore shared concurrent jurisdiction on many judicial matters. Sitting as a judicial body, the General Court handled a wide range of legal matters, from the probate of wills to criminal trials, including those for murder and witchcraft. The governor and assistants sat as the bench. The deputies (representatives of the towns) sometimes served as the jury but were usually excluded altogether from judicial deliberation. The General Court, instead, impaneled juries of laymen to hear particular cases.

On the local level, in each town a "select court" had been established, composed of three to five selectmen, to hear all civil cases of forty shillings or less and all minor criminal cases. It was not until 1685 that county courts were established, one for each of the three counties, making the Plymouth court system more comprehensive. The county court, sitting twice a year, was given the power to hear and determine all civil and criminal cases except for divorce and crimes punishable by death, mutilation, or banishment.

When the General Court convened on June 1, 1675, the first order of business was a series of annual elections of the governor, assistants, deputies, and other governmental officials. But it was the trial of the three Wampanoags that excited the Plymouth people during the first week of June. The case was tried by a panel of eight judges (the governor and seven assistants), presided over by Governor Josiah Winslow, son of Massasoit's close friend.

The three Indian defendants, Tobias, Wampapaquan, and Mattashunnamo, had already been accused of the crime three months earlier, but while the other two men remained in custody in Plymouth, Tobias, one of Philip's counselors and an important Wampanoag leader, had been released on a bond given by Tuspaquin and his son, William. Significantly, Tuspaquin, the sachem of Nemsaket and Philip's brother-in-law, was bailing out a suspected murderer of his own son-in-law, John Sassamon, on a hundred-pound bond he posted by mortgaging his lands of over one hundred square miles.

Why did Tuspaquin offer bail for Tobias? In quite a contrast to seventeenth-century England, where strict statutory rules governed the right of the accused to be released on bail (confessed felons, thieves "openly defamed and known," and persons accused of murder, treason, arson, counterfeiting, prison breaking, or contempt were not bailable), the New England colonists made bail a positive basic right. They declared that all persons had a right to bail except those accused of a capital crime.

This liberal, lenient policy was partly a result of the fact that colonial jails were very few in number, inadequate, and expensive to maintain. In colonial society, moreover, the bailed man would be under the constant watchful eyes of neighbors and could not easily flee from his community. If he succeeded in escaping to another town, he would be quickly suspected as a stranger. Pending trial, those released on bail could return to their community and resume their normal activities. This colonial system is said to have rested on "widespread confidence in the magistrates," who were in charge of deciding who were to be bailable, and the magistrates' "similar confidence in the townspeople, even in alleged criminals, relying on the suspect's sense of responsibility."

The New England colonies, by making bail a basic right and more crimes bailable, greatly improved the English practice. Except in "Crimes Capital, and Contempts in open Court," no man who would "put in sufficient securitie, bayle or mainprise, for his appearance and good behaviour in the meane time," said the Body of Liberties of Massachusetts of 1641, was to "be restrained or imprisoned by any Authority whatsoever, before the law hath sentenced him thereto."

Despite the positive improvement over English law, all the laws in New England colonies, which were basically similar, stipulated that those accused of capital offenses and repeaters of some other offenses would stay in jail. Why, then, was Tobias, who was accused of committing a nonbailable crime, allowed to post bail? The surety to post bail for Tobias was the sachem Tuspaquin, who, to the Plymouth authorities, was a trustworthy, important man who had been promoting the interests of the Christian church in his sachemship. No doubt Tuspaquin, a brother-in-law and staunch supporter of Philip, was doing whatever he could to help him, and was willing to post bail for Philip's close advisor, whom Tuspaquin probably knew well personally. The Plymouth authorities must have been reasonably confident that they were not taking any chances if they would allow Tuspaquin to post a huge bond and let him guarantee Tobias's good behavior during his release.

At their trial, none of the Wampanoag defendants was assisted by lawyers, however. Under English common law, felony defendants were not permitted the benefit of counsel, nor could counsel cross-examine witnesses or address the jury, but could only raise legal points for the court's consideration. The New England colonists improved the English practice by recognizing the right to counsel as one of the important rights guaranteed to the criminal defendant since the early seventeenth century. In Massachusetts, the Body of Liberties guaranteed the right to counsel without restriction as to the nature of the offense. "Every man that findeth himself unfit to plead his owne cause in any Court," states Article 26, "shall have Liberties to imploy any man against whom the Court doth not except, to helpe him, Provided he give him noe fee or reward for his pains." Rhode Island went further when it enacted in 1644 that defendants had the right to counsel and that each town should maintain two attorneys for whoever would need them, "discreet, honest and able men for understanding," who would be chosen by the townsmen and would "belong to the Court." Despite these guarantees, however, the advantage of having unpaid attorneys was seldom claimed during the seventeenth century. The general custom of consulting lawyers over legal matters was not yet well established, and criminal defendants were generally often not represented by counsel.

(In the witchcraft trials of 1692, for example, none of the defendants had the benefit of a lawyer, and every accused witch was found guilty.)

The situation seems to have been worse in the case of Indians, many of whom were tried before the colonial courts without an attorney representing them. In theory, legal counsel was available to everyone, but in practice, the natives did not (or could not) make use of their rights to the fullest extent. In comparison with the English settlers, Indian defendants enjoyed the aid of counsel only in a limited way, and they often confessed with little pressure.

In capital cases, however, the Indian defendants did usually have the privilege of having lawyers to defend their cases. For reasons not clearly stated in the records, Tobias and his two co-defendants did not ask for lawyers, nor were any lawyers assigned to them. The Sassamon murder case is one of the few exceptions in colonial New England in which a capital case was tried without defense counsel. Yet as in all the serious criminal cases, of both colonists and Indian defendants, his Majesty's attorney was appointed to prosecute the Sassamon case.

In 1685, when an Indian named James Morgan was convicted of murdering an Englishman, was sentenced to death, but abandoned his right to appeal, he had an English lawyer named Vaughan. Vaughan presented Morgan's petition to the court, in which he admitted his sinful life, acknowledged the justness of the decision, and expressed a desire for a longer time to live, but it was denied. In 1711, a Boston Indian woman named Maria was probably the only Indian who was successfully defended by her counsel on her charge, in which she was accused of murdering her illegitimate child. The able defense by her master, William Hutchinson, convinced the jury to return the verdict of not guilty. When an Indian, named George Necho of Wells, York County (present-day Maine), was indicted in 1740 for raping a three-year-old English girl, he was found guilty and sentenced to death. Then his English lawyer tried to secure the benefit of clergy (the privilege of being spared the death penalty if a convicted criminal could read a particular verse from the Bible) for him, but to no avail. He was executed three weeks later.

By the end of the century, as colonial society gradually grew into maturity and became more complex, lawyers were beginning to assume a prominent role and gaining some recognition as professionals, although the legal profession did not fully develop until the first half of the eighteenth century.

At the end of the seventeenth century, when the use of an attorney became more common and criminal defendants began to realize that having an attorney was a great advantage, the Indians as well as the settlers started to use lawyers to defend their cases.

Trial by jury was another fundamental right accorded to every criminal defendant in all colonial courts except the justice of the peace (magistrate) courts, which employed "summary procedure," the judge ruling without jury. The Indians could equally enjoy trial by jury, although native defendants did not always exercise this right. Although the majority of jurors for Indian trials were Englishmen, the records reveal some natives serving as jurymen. In 1674, for example, the jury in a Massachusetts Court of Assistants case that returned the verdict of guilty on a rape charge for an Indian named Tom, who was eventually sentenced to death, consisted of six Indians and six whites.

In the Sassamon murder trial, the jury impaneled consisted of twelve regular Englishmen and six of the "most indefferentest, gravest, and sage Indians." These Indian jurors (named Hope, Maskippague, Wannoo, George, Wampye, and Acanootus), who were all Praying Indians, supplemented, rather than substituted for, the regular English jurymen. Their function was "to healp to consult and advice with, of, and concerning the premises."

The jury impaneled for the trial of the three Wampanoag defendants was certainly not a jury of their peers, because none of the Indian jurors was chosen from the Wampanoags under Philip. Some historians, therefore, have gone so far as to argue that these Indians were added to the jury because, unlike the defendants, they were Christian Indians, and their selection would serve "to drive a wedge between Philip's pagans and Plymouth's converts, to make reconciliation between them impossible under any circumstances." The Plymouth court, however, might have selected the Indian jurors from the Praying Indians as the best candidates to participate in the English administration of justice at the trial of Indians, including hostile Indians, because they were "civilized" and thus were more familiar with colonial law and its operation and yet still understood the traditional Indian way of life.

The trial centered around the testimony of the prosecution's star witness, an Indian by the name of Patuckson. He testified that he was standing behind a tree on a hill near the shore of the pond when the attack on Sassamon took place. Patuckson claimed that these three of Philip's men had violently assaulted and murdered Sassamon and tried to conceal their crime by throwing his body through a hole in the ice, making it look like an accidental death. The records, however, are not detailed enough to know the extent of Patuckson's testimony.

To what extent the colonists relied on Indian testimony in the courts in New England was a controversial issue, especially in the eighteenth century, when the popular prejudice against Indians (which actually began in 1675 as a direct result of King Philip's War) became more pronounced, creating a tendency to discredit them as competent witnesses. There were, however, no statutory restrictions on Indian testimony during most of the seventeenth century. Despite occasional doubts expressed by some colonists about the validity of native testimony on the ground that the Indians would not understand the swearing of an oath on the Bible, their testimony was generally admitted as fully as that of English settlers.

In 1674, just one year before the trial, the Plymouth court in another case involving Indians charged its juries to give full credence to native testimony in all cases "as [if] it were the testimony of an Englishman, whether the Indian had sworn an oath on the Bible or not." Thus Patuckson's testimony had to be made fully admissible, but his credibility as a witness became suddenly shaky when it was revealed that Patuckson had personal motives for accusing the defendants: he owed them a gambling debt. When the Indian witness showed the court a coat, blaming the defendants for giving it to him in order to conceal the murder they had committed, these suspects retorted that Patuckson had played away his coat, but they returned it to him not to keep him quiet, but to demand instead the payment of his debt. But Patuckson, the defendants insisted, instead of paying back, "accused them, and knowing it would please the English so to think him a better Christian." It was also testified in the trial by some other Indian that John Sassamon, before he died, had expressed his fears that those very Indians would be his death.

Nevertheless, the Plymouth General Court not only accepted Patuckson's testimony as valid but also decided to convict the defendants solely on the testimony of one Indian witness. This move was quite contrary to the general principle established in the seventeenth-century New England colonies that a minimum of two witnesses was required for conviction in capital cases. Coincidentally, the Plymouth court was seriously deviating from its own normal procedural rule in a Wampanoag case at the very time when "public feeling against the Wampanoags was running high." Quite naturally, King Philip severely criticized the sincerity of Plymouth justice.

At any rate, the guilty verdict the regular English jurors reached based solely upon Patuckson's testimony was fully concurred with by the Indian jurors. The verdict reads:

> We, of the jury, one and all, both English and Indians, doe joyntly and width one consent agree upon a verdict: that Tobias, and his son Wampapaquan, and Mattashunnamo, the Indians, whoe are the prisoners, are guilty of the blood of John Sassamon, and were the murderers of him, according to the bill of indi[c]t[e]ment.

The court then sentenced the three Wampanoags "to be hanged by the head until theire bodies are dead" on June 8, 1675, although the Indians still vehemently maintained their innocence. In accordance with the Plymouth law, the lands and other real and personal properties belonging to the convicted Wampanoags were confiscated.

One of the major objectives of colonial court procedure throughout English North America was a speedy determination of the truth in both criminal and civil affairs. The New England colonies strictly adhered to this rule by guaranteeing it in the laws and statutes they passed. Most of the criminal cases were heard within one to three months after the indictment, and such a privilege was fully assured to the Indians. Criminal sentences (including death by hanging) were also swiftly carried out, usually within two or three months. At times, however, death sentences were carried out more promptly. In the case of four Mohawks who killed Richard Church, a Hadley, Massachusetts, resident, on October 5, 1696, a special Court of Oyer and Terminer tried them for murder on October 21. Two of them as the principals were shot to death two days after sentencing. The three Wampanoags were scheduled to die only one week after they were sentenced for murdering John Sassamon.

On the scheduled day of the execution, June 8, John Cotton preached to the Indians who had gathered at Plymouth to witness the hanging. In the executions that followed, an unusual thing happened. After the first two of the condemned Indians, Tobias and Mattashunnamo, were duly put to death, the last to die, Tobias's son, Wampapaquan, was swung into the air. His rope, however, snapped, knocking him to the ground. The terrified Wampapaquan, who had been thus far asserting his innocence as the other two did to the very end, now decided to talk for the possibility of a reprieve. He confessed that the three were indeed responsible for the murder, but he insisted that the other two did the actual killing while he himself was "no actor in it, yet a looker on." He also implicated Philip in the murder, suggesting that the sachem had ordered Sassamon's death.

Despite the failed execution, which usually exempted the condemned from further punishment, and a promised pardon in exchange for his confession, the Plymouth authorities were unwilling to relieve Wampapaquan. One month later, Plymouth decided to try his execution again. By then the war, which started by the skirmishes at Swansea, was already in full swing. Hanging was the only form of capital punishment sanctioned in the New England colonies, although other means of execution were employed on rare, extraordinary occasions. The Plymouth authorities made sure that nothing would go wrong on the second try by shooting Wampapaquan to death.

The trial, conviction, and execution of the three Wampanoags for murdering John Sassamon marked the end of the old relationship and the beginning of a new era between the Plymouth colony and the Wampanoags. For the colonists, the transition may not have been so apparent: it was part of the gradual territorial, economic, and political expansion stimulated by population growth, leading to closer contacts and resultant conflicts between the two cultures.

For the Wampanoags, however, the change was sudden, drastic, and disturbing. Why were the Wampanoags forced to allow Plymouth colony to handle the death of John Sassamon, instead of being able to solve such an internal problem in their own way? Philip and his Wampanoags not only objected to Plymouth's handling the matter but were infuriated by the way the colony handled it. The issue was the Wampanoags' autonomy, which was now in serious jeopardy.

CHAPTER 8

The Wampanoag Story

The death of John Sassamon exposed an irreconcilable problem evolving from jurisdictional conflict between two drastically different legal cultures. The conflict of law, the rule to decide which nation's law should be applied to particular cases arising from legal relations between two nations, was a relatively easy problem among European nations, which adhered to basically the same legal tradition and system.

The Sassamon case, in which Plymouth colony and the Wampanoags were involved, presented a problem that was not the simple jurisdictional issue of who would have the authority to try the case, but a controversy touching their entire legal systems and laws. For the Wampanoags to allow the Plymouth colony to handle the Sassamon case, instead of being able to solve it by themselves in their own way, was surely to undermine and jeopardize their cultural, social, and legal traditions.

How did the Wampanoags look at the whole event? While the Plymouth authorities insisted that the Sassamon murder case should be handled by the Plymouth court because the incident took place within the jurisdiction of Plymouth colony (the principle of *territoriality*), the Wampanoags argued that the death of Sassamon was no one's business but theirs because the incident appeared to involve only members of their group, regardless of where it took place (the principle of *personality*).

Among the Wampanoags there were doubts about whether Sassamon had indeed been murdered; some maintained that Sassamon fell into the water and was drowned, hurting his throat on the ice. Even those who would concede that the death of Sassamon was a homicide firmly believed that the Wampanoags would not have handled the case the way the Plymouth court had done.

In contrast to English law practiced in Plymouth and other English North American colonies, which made murder an offense against the state and made the state responsible for apprehending, putting on trial, and punishing the murderer, the Wampanoags treated a homicide as a private, personal, clan matter. It had to be decided, as all other legal matters were decided, according to Indian retributive justice. Murder was an offense against the victim's clan, and therefore it was the clan's obligation to deal with the offender. The entire clan was responsible for the commission of homicide, and the clan had the duty and function to carry out the punishment for homicide.

The murder of John Sassamon was thus a problem between Sassamon's clan and the murderers' clans. When Philip went to Plymouth in March 1675 and voluntarily appeared before the General Court, he was trying not only to clear himself, insisting that he had no role in Sassamon's death, but also more importantly to negotiate with the Plymouth authorities for the transfer of the three Wampanoag prisoners to him, because he believed that Plymouth had no authority to handle the problem, which was a Wampanoag internal problem and had nothing to do with Plymouth. He had little success; he could not erase the Plymouth authorities' doubt about his innocence, nor was he able to persuade them that he had the right to take the Wampanoag prisoners back home and deal with them according to their own law. He was only able to secure the release of Tobias on an excessive bail, pending trial in Plymouth!

It was a prerogative of the sachem to discipline, punish, or even kill the persons who had acted against the interest of the group or its sachem. If Philip had his men kill Sassamon, who had betrayed him and informed the Plymouth authorities that the Wampanoag sachem had been planning to make war against the English, he was simply exercising his authority as the sachem to protect the group, without being liable to anyone.

King Philip could carry out this power over Sassamon, even though Philip was the maternal uncle of Sassamon's wife, a relationship that usually had an exceptionally close tie of consanguinity in the Algonquian family. It is not likely, however, that Philip was responsible for the death of Sassamon. Earlier, in 1671, when Sassamon informed Plymouth that Philip had been entertaining some Narragansett and other sachems, trying to recruit their support for his plot to exterminate or drive the English settlers away from the country, Philip was summoned to Plymouth to answer the charges. Philip must have been extremely angry, but he did not do anything to Sassamon then.

The authorities of the New England colonies, including Plymouth, had long recognized the power of the sachem to restrain, sanction, punish, and even kill any member of his band who would act against the interest of the sachem, in both personal and official capacities. In fact, there had been a well-established tradition among the colonies of accepting such functions as a legitimate exercise of the sachem's power. All sides were fully familiar with several important precedents that had been set in this regard. The supposed poisoning of Wyandanch, a sachem of the Montauk of Long Island, for example, was left to the Indians themselves and was never brought to trial by the English.

In 1643, the Narragansett chief sachem Miantonomo allegedly hired one of the Mohegans' Pequot wards to assassinate Uncas. After his arrow failed to kill Uncas, only slightly wounding his arm, the assassin fled to the Narragansetts for protection. When Uncas took his complaint to the commissioners of the New England Confederation, Miantonomo and his Pequot suspect were summoned to Boston to answer the charge. Though the testimony the Pequot gave in Miantonomo's presence contradicted what he gave in his absence, the United Colonies authorities decided to release both of them pending further investigation. On their way home, Miantonomo simply beheaded his accomplice, the star witness for the English, but the commissioners never imposed any sanction against the Narragansett sachem.

Later the same year, Miantonomo invaded the Mohegan territory with a thousand men. When the Narragansett chief was captured by Uncas and was turned over to the English, the United Colonies commissioners turned him back over to Uncas, ordering him to kill Miantonomo. Uncas was instructed to take him out of English jurisdiction and to murder him in Mohegan territory. The English thus not only allowed but also endorsed an Indian chief to dispose of another chief as he saw fit in his own country. The English even sent a group of soldiers with Uncas to protect him after Miantonomo's sanctioned murder.

The English practice of approving Indians' executing other Indians, instead of taking the matter into their own hands, continued even during wartime. As late as April 1676, Canonchet (Nananawtunu), the youngest son of Miantonomo, who had assumed a strong leadership position over the Narragansetts during King Philip's War, was captured by a combined force of Connecticut militia and Indians. When Canonchet chose death with dignity, rejecting an offer to live in peace with the English, his execution was done solely by Indians, not by English. He fell before the Mohegan firing squad led by Uncas's oldest son, Tatuphosuwut (better known as Oweneco), and his body was later mutilated by the Mohegans.

Toward the end of the war, in July 1675, a spectacular mass surrender of about 180 Nipmucks took place in Boston. They were brought by a prominent Nipmuck, Sagamore John. Among the prisoners were the much-wanted sachem Matoonas, who had led the first attack on a Massachusetts town (Mendon) in the war. Matoonas was taken to Boston Common, where he was tied to a tree. It was Sagamore John and his men who shot their fellow Nipmuck to death.

For the Wampanoag Indians, whose legal system was based upon the principle of *personality* and who considered that there had been well-established precedent in the matter, what Plymouth did was not in accordance with the generally accepted policy of the New England colonies. Instead of trying the murder suspects by its law, Plymouth should have let Philip handle it. It was decisively arbitrary, unreasonable, and high-handed. Plymouth made no earnest efforts to negotiate with the Wampanoag sachem as had been customarily done in the past in such a case. The decision of Plymouth authorities to punish Philip's people for any crime was a clear violation of the agreement guaranteed in the treaties since 1621.

The Plymouth Treaty of 1621, concluded between Governor

John Carver and Massasoit, presupposed mutual respect for their legal jurisdictions between a powerful Indian nation and a small number of colonists who had just started a settlement in an area surrounded by Indians. The provisions were, therefore, not the Pilgrims' unilateral demands on the Indians to accept the English law but their requests to respect their own society. It was an immunity from the Indian legal system that the colonists were seeking, not a give-and-take arrangement.

The main agreements the Pilgrims secured—no injuries or harms would be done to the English by Massasoit and his people, no weapons would be brought into the English settlement, and the Indian offenders against the English would be brought to Plymouth for punishment—were all concessions from the Wampanoags. Massasoit did not allow the colonists to extend Plymouth's jurisdiction over the Indian country. He simply permitted the English law to prevail over matters arising among the English and from Indian-English relations within their colony, the limited area of English settlements and their surroundings.

The Pilgrims were not interested in forcing English law on the Indians, but were trying to protect their own society by taking the colonists out of the sphere of Indian control. This agreement continued through the renewed treaties until the early 1640s.

As the English population increased and settlements grew in size and in number, colonial jurisdiction expanded accordingly. Yet the basic arrangement of legal coexistence between the Pilgrims and the Wampanoags continued to prevail, and the Indians continued to maintain their autonomy and their independence from the English.

Beginning in the 1640s, the Plymouth authorities came increasingly to believe that the English, whether they were in their own territory or on Indian land, should be subject to their own law and court, thus insisting in a sense on their extraterritorial rights in the Indian country. On the other hand, the English denied such rights to the Indians, who had in fact been practicing it all along among the tribes themselves, based upon the principle that the Indian group had jurisdiction over its members within or without its territory, the principle of personality.

The colonial authorities also began to demand delivery to the colony of Indian offenders in crimes committed against the English outside colonial jurisdiction. But they were not always successful, simply because the Indians refused, insisting that such deliveries would jeopardize their political and jurisdictional independence and autonomy.

Until 1675, the Indians stood at least on the same footing as the English, maintaining their independence, and legal co-existence prevailed, despite various disputes arising between them. Mutual agreement on the independence of the Indian nation and the colony and mutual respect for the jurisdiction of the other were the basic policies of both sides established by the early treaties. Subsequent treaties between the Plymouth authorities and the Wampanoags, especially the one of 1671, somewhat altered this relationship, but the basic rule of co-existence that had been set forth earlier remained unchanged until the death of John Sassamon—at least the Wampanoags thought so.

Before 1675, many of the intercultural legal problems had been settled by negotiation, arbitration, and compromises, based upon mutual respect of each other's jurisdiction. The Peach case of 1638 is the best example, in which the question of who should handle the case was decided by the representatives of Massachusetts Bay and Plymouth and Indian leaders, including Miantonomo, who at first demanded delivery of the suspects. They agreed that the Plymouth court should hear the case because the murder took place in Plymouth and was committed apparently by Plymouth settlers. The Indians were, however, assured that the Plymouth court would try the defendants fairly and justly. Some Narragansett and Wampanoag sachems, including Massasoit, attended the trial, in which the accused, confronted with solid evidence against them, confessed their guilt. In the end, some of the Narragansetts were invited to Plymouth and witnessed the execution of the offenders, in place of personal revenge against the offenders. Some maintained that Plymouth could not afford not to have a fair trial, given the precarious situation the colonies were in during the late 1630s. If the colony had ignored the crime, the Narragansetts might have declared war.

This case is quite a contrast to the Sassamon case, which had only one witness, who was seriously discredited by the defendants. Nor were the influential Wampanoag sachems like Philip invited to the trial.

The southern New England Indians were not very successful in convincing the colonial authorities to hand over to them cases of an intercultural nature, but Indian chiefs and the victims' relatives were often invited at public expense to the trials of the English against the Indians to see justice done, although they at times were astonished to see the juries return not-guilty verdicts. Yet significantly, the colonial authorities made efforts to maintain good relations with the Indians through negotiation in legal conflicts. In May 1671, when an Indian murdered a Bay Colony colonist and the Boston authorities asked Philip to help apprehend the suspect, Philip fully complied and played an "industriously active" role in bringing him to justice.

More important, the very idea that the colonial court could try the cases of Indian crimes against Indians committed within the colonial jurisdiction was utterly unacceptable to the Wampanoags, who adhered to the principle of personality. The colonists' view that all the accused, including Indians, must be tried at the court in the area where the crime was committed had in fact already been challenged even by some colonists.

William Pynchon of Springfield, for example, fully took the Indian legal tradition into consideration when he denied in 1648 that Massachusetts Bay Colony magistrates could rightly apprehend and pass judgment on several Indians in western Massachusetts who had allegedly murdered other Indians. Although the crime had been committed "within the line of the patent," these Indians were, he argued, not within the Massachusetts jurisdiction because they had not fully subjected themselves to the colonial government. Until their land be bought, he insisted, these Indians should "be esteemed as an independent free people." Significantly, this is the principle that many Indians including Philip had been insisting on.

As late as 1675, just a little before the Sassamon case was heard, Uncas's oldest son, Oweneco, was brought before a Connecticut court for murdering a Narragansett sachem, Johne-quam. Oweneco pleaded self-defense, claiming the victim had as-saulted him with a knife. He also stated that Johnequam "had threatened to murther uncass and so might have a grudge against his son to make such an assult upon him in his stead." Just a few days before the sentence was to be passed upon Oweneco, when the three Wampanoag defendants had already been convicted in Plymouth, Roger Williams in a letter written to John Winthrop Jr., the governor of Connecticut, confidently predicted that Oweneco would suffer the same fate as the three convicted Wampanoags. But a deal was struck between the Connecticut court and the Mohegans. On June 18, the court dropped the case for lack of sufficient evidence, released Oweneco to the custody of his father, Uncas, and warned the Mohegans against commit-ting any such acts in the future. Why was such a deal never struck between Plymouth and the Wampanoags? No effort had ever been made to negotiate on the part of the Plymouth authorities in the Sassamon case. In the trial, there was no active participa-tion by either Philip, his counselors, or other Wampanoag lead-ers. In fact, not only were there no attempts and offers of negotiation and reconciliation, or deals, but the records show no Wampanoags were ever invited to witness the open trial or to testify for the defendants. Did the Plymouth leaders realize by then that they had reached the point of no return, and they had to deal with the problem as they saw fit, without ever hearing the other side's story or ever consulting them?

To the Wampanoags, the Sassamon case was rigged from the start. Were the Plymouth authorities really serious in providing equal justice to the Wampanoags? Or did Plymouth have no in-tention of according such treatment to Philip's men?

King Philip and his Wampanoags, even when they were forced to concede the aggressive decision of the Pilgrims to try the case before the Plymouth court, did have a slight hope, but quickly discovered that the Plymouth court would not live up to its own basic standard. It failed to extend to the Wampanoags the rights guaranteed to English defendants and a fair trial. The Ply-mouth authorities in fact, by taking the case forcefully into their own hands on the pretext of rendering a just decision, used their court system to make a political decision, seriously deviating from regular court procedure.

The very assertion that Sassamon had been murdered was highly questionable and should have been challenged more thoroughly. The theory many Indians held, that Sassamon fell into the water accidentally and drowned, had never been fully investigated. Could the twelve-member jury of inquest, which was drawn from the residents of a small frontier town in the middle of the Wampanoag country but included no single Indian, arrive at an objective, fair, and impartial conclusion without any undue pressure and influence?

There is nothing more common among the populace who crowd around the bodies of persons found dead than to suspect that they have been murdered, but sudden death is not an uncommon event. Persistent rumors of conspiracies against the English had been heard, conspiracies supposedly instigated by Philip and his men, who were living in the nearby region. Was it possible that these inquest jurors, faced with Sassamon's body, jumped to a conclusion because they already had prejudice, fear, and hostility toward the Indians? Such preconceived notions could have tarnished their ability to examine the body objectively.

Although colonial law stipulated that criminal defendants had a right to be represented by lawyers, the three Wampanoags did not have the opportunity to have lawyers defending their case. Having counsel was obviously a great advantage, but why could the Wampanoags not exercise this right? Was the right denied to them? Did they waive the right to counsel? Or could they not afford to hire lawyers even if they wanted them? Weren't public defenders available to them?

The Plymouth court records state that the Indian defendants strongly maintained their innocence throughout the trial. What did they specifically say in their defense? Certainly, without counsel they could not have presented their case effectively. Counsel could argue the law to the bench, they could challenge the prosecution, they could call witnesses on behalf of the defendants and cross-examine hostile witnesses, and they could address juries effectively and persuasively; ordinary defendants, especially those three Wampanoags, could not do well by themselves.

The colonial laws guaranteed jury trials in criminal cases as well as civil suits. The Pilgrims, who were the first English settlers in New England to pass a law stipulating that all facts in criminal cases were to be determined by juries, failed in securing impartial justice to the Wampanoag defendants. The New England colonies at first followed the English practice of appointing juries, but gradually juries came to be elected, and sometimes chosen by lot. In New England, defendants commonly asked for a jury trial, but when defendants in capital cases declined a jury trial, the judge usually forced them to change their pleas to "not guilty" so that they could have the jury trial in order to ensure complete justice.

Obviously, a jury trial did not necessarily guarantee a better outcome for the defendant. Juries indeed convicted defendants as often as they acquitted them. The three Wampanoag defendants were guaranteed a trial by jury to be sure, but they faced a very hostile jury, which was by no means a jury of their peers. Not only the regular English jurors but the auxiliary jury of six Indians, who were Christian Indians, did not represent the community the defendants came from. The defendants did not share values and views with these Praying Indian jurors, whom the defendants and other tribesmen looked down upon with hatred, resentment, and contempt.

Above all, it was an inexcusable and serious mistake for the Plymouth court to convict Philip's three men of murdering Sassamon and sentence them to death on the testimony of only one Indian witness. When Patuckson gave his testimony in direct confrontation with Tobias and the other two accused, his credibility came to be severely questioned. The defendants firmly believed that Patuckson had been bribed to give false testimony against them and that the defendants had been framed for a murder that had never been committed, since Sassamon had actually drowned.

Nor did Patuckson's testimony exactly and definitely collaborate the findings of the coroner's inquest. At any rate, convicting a person and giving a death sentence on the testimony of one witness was the most flagrant violation of the Plymouth bill of rights. The first chapter of the Plymouth *Colony Book of General Laws*, enacted in 1672, which was partly the compilation of various laws already in force, did guarantee a bill of rights, including equal and impartial administration of justice and rights, the right of all men to a jury trial, the right of the defendant to challenge the jury for cause, the right to preemptory challenge in a capital crime, and the prohibition of a death sentence without the testimony of at least two witnesses unless there was "other sufficient Evidence or Circumstances equivalent thereunto."

The *Book of Laws* declared that these rights were "so Fundamentally essential to the just Rights, Liberties, Common good and special end of this Colony, as that they shall and ought to be inviolably preserved." Why, then, weren't Tobias and his two codefendants accorded the rights that the Plymouth colonists valued so highly? Was this guarantee intended to safeguard only the colonists, not the Indians, even when they were tried before the Plymouth court? Here, to the Wampanoags, Plymouth's sincerity was seriously questioned.

What did the Wampanoags think about Sassamon's broken neck, which had been allegedly considered to be the cause of the death? The statement of Increase Mather that Sassamon had been killed by a broken neck caused by the "twisting of his head around," which was "the way that the Indians some times use when they practice murthers" is simply false. The twisting of the neck was by no means a typical method the Indians used to kill people. Since it would require an excessive amount of force and violence to kill an individual in this way, it was not very commonly used by the Indians. The Indians employed, instead, a variety of other, more common, means to murder individuals: stabbing, shooting, strangling, splitting the head open with a hatchet, beheading, and poisoning.

According to the official records, Patuckson testified that the three defendants shoved Sassamon's body into the pond through a hole in the ice in order to conceal the murder. They may very well have killed Sassamon by throwing him into the water alive, but it was not the Wampanoag way—or at least would be an unusual act for Indians—to throw a dead body into the water to conceal a murder. Some may argue that the murderers were trying to conceal their act not only from the English but also from the wrath of Philip. The killing could have been done by Tobias and his confederates, who hated Sassamon and much detested what he was, without the knowledge of Philip, who would not want to kill the husband of his favored niece. But if the murderers were trying to conceal their act by throwing Sassmon's body in the water under the ice, they did not do a good job. They neglected to hide Sassamon's hat, gun, and brace of ducks, and left them on the ice. In any case, under their law of homicide, there was no compelling reason for the Indians to conceal their murderous acts.

And alas! What about Tobias's son, Wampapaquan? Men were expected not only to be loyal, adventurous, and independent but also to be brave and to endure pain without flinching or crying out. This boy was no brave. He was so shaken by the whole incident that he decided to say anything that the Plymouth authorities wanted to hear to save his life. A man was supposed to go through such an ordeal with a show of outward calm. It was an unspeakable disgrace for him to act the way he did. Wampapaquan, nevertheless, should have been excused from further punishment when his execution was not consummated. The failed execution obviously should have entitled him to a pardon, but here again the Plymouth court's decision to try his execution again after the promise of reprieve was cruel. Such English behavior, however, did not surprise the Indians.

During the past forty years, it had proven abundantly clear in their dealing with them that the English colonists were ruthless, cruel, brutal, and revengeful. In the Pequot War, when the English massacred three hundred to seven hundred Pequots, including women and children, at Mystic Fort in May 1637, it shocked the Indians as well as many colonists. Later in the war, two Pequot sachems surrendered with many warriors but were spared their lives for their possible assistance in locating the remaining Pequots. Despite their willing cooperation with the English war efforts, these sachems were in the end executed. How could the English justify killing them simply because they hadn't been, after all, very helpful!

The English role in instigating intertribal conflict between the Mohegan sachem Uncas and the Narragansetts, and eventually taking the side of the Mohegans by attacking the Narragansetts in 1643, is a clear manifestation of English perfidy that many Indians might have long remembered. They were fierce, uncompromising, dictatorial, and determined to punish the Indians.

In dealing with the Indians, the English often resorted to such unusually harsh and cruel sanctions and punishment, not common among the European nations. Such exaggerated and excessive actions were in part designed to teach the Indians lessons, although the Indians were, as was shown abundantly throughout the colonial period, not easily cowed by such treatment.

How did King Philip respond to the decision of the Plymouth court? Philip and his men must have been boiling with deep resentment and anger about the verdicts and the executions of three of their people. Why did the executions have to be performed so swiftly? Didn't the defendants have the right to appeal or review? The guilty verdict for the three Wampanoags, fully concurred with by the Indian jurors, had the appearance of fairness, impartiality, and complete justice, but it was merely the product of the Plymouth authorities, who used their tribunal to force Philip and the Wampanoags to conform, and by so doing they grossly undermined their own legal principles.

Many colonists might simply have believed that Philip was alarmed and disturbed by Plymouth's active prosecution of the Sassamon case, fearing that his own role as instigator of the crime would be revealed. But such was not his concern. Philip must have realized that his own legal independence and autonomy was at stake. Philip maintained, as did the Narragansett sachems Pessacus and Canonicus in the 1640s, that the Indian tribes and the English colonies were equally subjects of the king of England. He asserted the independence of the Wampanoags from Plymouth and flatly denied its authority to intervene in his internal affairs, in either intra- or intertribal matters, and to punish his people for any crime.

{ *Igniting King Philip's War* }

CHAPTER 9

And the War Came

The Wampanoags took the decision in the Sassamon case as a great grievance. It was not because the incident was itself important, but because of the larger implications of the case. What emerged in the courtroom, and in the executions that followed, was more than a routine clash of legal cultures; rather, it was the intense cultural tension and deep mistrust that had developed between Plymouth and the Wampanoags.

What did the Sassamon case really entail? First, Plymouth took over the case from the Wampanoags, who had the proper and legitimate power to handle it themselves. They then tried the case according to their own law, not taking the Wampanoag law into consideration. There was no negotiation, mediation, or arbitration on the jurisdictional and other matters. Nor were any Wampanoag leaders invited to attend the trial. At the trial, no full reports on Sassamon's body were available simply because the body had not been examined thoroughly to ascertain the real cause of his death. Forensic medicine was not very advanced, but an autopsy could have been performed by some specialist who could have been summoned from a neighboring colony. Moreover, the Plymouth authorities did not even comply with their own law, but seriously deviated from it.

Legal coexistence, which had long been observed by both cultures, came gradually to be undermined by a series of mediations and compromises that settled specific incidents and cases, deviating from the basic rule and principle. But it was the Sassamon case that suddenly and flatly destroyed the principle of legal coexistence, forcing the Indians to conform to the English law.

What Plymouth had done was to decide the case to serve its purpose and promote its own interest, at the expense of Wampanoag fundamental rights. It was very evident to the Wampanoags that the colony was advancing its selfish interests and objectives in the name of justice. Before the case was finally decided, Philip might have hoped that the Plymouth/Wampanoag relations could improve. But this decision clearly demonstrated that there would be no such possibilities.

From then on, Philip feared the Plymouth authorities would continue to force the Indians to conform in every other aspect of law until they would lose their autonomy entirely. This decision was not limited to legal encroachment; it was merely a legal manifestation of the wholesale encroachment upon the Wampanoags.

Historians have repeatedly identified numerous factors that eventually led to King Philip's War: English hunger for Indian lands, uncontrolled growth of the colonial settlement, English racial prejudice toward the Indians, arrogance of Plymouth leaders, aggressive Christian missionary activities, trade abuses, and mutual misunderstandings of concepts of land ownership, life philosophies, and social norms.

Behind all these forces, however, a clear trend had been emerging: the growing power and influence of the English at the expense of the Indians, whose control was rapidly declining. The English were now increasingly dominating the political, economic, social, and cultural life of the Wampanoag country, which was growing alarmingly smaller.

The acceptance of the Sassamon decision, therefore, meant to the Indians their giving up not only legal but political, economic, and cultural independence. It was these pressures on Indian autonomy that culminated in the outbreak of King Philip's War.

Diplomacy came also to be conducted in the manner dictated by the colonists. Colonial authorities never visited Mount Hope to conduct negotiations, but instead the sachem had to travel to Plymouth. The colonists became more aggressive in demanding the Wampanoags to yield, while they themselves would never yield. Mediation failed, almost always because of the colonists' unwillingness to compromise. The Sassamon case abundantly proved that the English dominance and pressure were not merely a trend but a reality.

The Plymouth government was no longer functioning as friend or protector, but instead it was turning into a predator, and the Wampanoags realized that they no longer had anyone to promote their interests with the Plymouth government. The future, to Philip, seemed bleak. The problems and conflicts the Wampanoags had been having, such as English settlements nearby, livestock, and land, had to be understood in the context of the Sassamon decision.

A few days after two of the convicted Wampanoags had been executed, John Easton, the Quaker deputy governor of Rhode Island, met Philip for possible arbitration. Philip responded by pointing out his grievances. Philip, for example, attacked the colonial fencing policy, which had been causing serious damage to his villages. "Even after they sold land," he stated, Indians suffered because "the English Catell and horses still incresed that when they removed 30 mill from wher English had anithing to do, they Could not kepe ther coren from being spoyled." He said that "when the English boft [bought] land of them," the Wampanoags had expected "that thay would have kept ther Catell upon ther owned land."

The fence problem between England and Indians was the result of the unique policy the colonists adopted in the New World. Departing from English law, which made the owner responsible for the damage done by his animal, the colonial legislatures and courts throughout North America imposed upon the landowner a duty to fence his field against trespassing cattle. No damages were recoverable if this requirement was not met. The purpose of this policy was partly to increase the meager supply of livestock by permitting cattle to wander about in vast, open fields in order to breed faster. Damage by cattle gave constant problems not only to the Indians but also to the English. The colonists, instead of constructing expensive fences, took such measures as driving invading livestock to a river and letting them drown, or simply shooting them. Many went to court to recover damages, but a landowner who failed to meet the standards prescribed by the fence statute could not as plaintiff recover damages.

{ *And the War Came* }   127

Indians were treated differently and were accorded practical compromises. Efforts to make the law equitable to the Indians, however, did not always work. Finally in 1667, Plymouth passed a law providing that those Englishmen whose horses and cattle might trespass upon Indians' lands and spoil their corn should "agree with them" to help them to construct fences. If they neglected to assist the Indians to fence, they would be required to pay the full damage to the Indians themselves. This law of fencing clearly recognized the Indian way of life and tried to protect their interest even at the expense of the English. But such protective measures were not usually familiar to the Indians. The Wampanoags, without realizing a special protection was accorded to them, simply believed that the standard law of fencing would apply to them as well as the settlers. The rigid enforcement of such a law, as the Plymouth authorities were doing in the case of Sassamon's death, the Wampanoags feared, would be very harmful to their interests. They simply took the invading cattle that devastated their fields as the forerunner of ruthless encroachment upon the Indian country by the government-sponsored English settlement.

The English method of establishing evidence also came under attack. Philip burst out at the Plymouth authorities for their hypocrisy, declaring, "They would never accept the testimony of 20 of the honest Indians, if they were against an Englishman for a wrong done to them, but they would never reject the testimony of even one of ther Worst indians, if it was against the sachem or his men."

The adverse decision in the Sassamon case was the result of this corrupt practice, and Philip feared that the Wampanoags would be forced to accept such practices as part of the Plymouth justice system.

Uncontrolled, ever-expanding English settlements were another serious problem. Philip protested that when "the English first Came . . . was . . . a litell Child," but Massasoit had "let them have a 100 times more land, then now the king had for his own." He then complained that when the sachems agreed to sell land, "the English wold say it was more than thay agred to and a writing must be prove [proof] against all them." If any sachem opposed such sales, the English would "make a nother king that wold give or sell them there land, that now theay had no hope left to kepe ani land." The Wampanoag land, as the result of such practices, continued to shrink. The situation became very serious in the Mount Hope area, where Philip lived, because the peninsula came to be blocked by increasing numbers of English settlements. The problem would be more pressing in the near future if more aggressive Plymouth policies were instituted to protect such settlements.

The Christian missionary activities were another of Philip's concerns. Christianization, which meant not only conversion but also Europeanization, would force the Indians to change their way of life, not only undermining the traditional Indian society and culture but threatening the power of the sachem. Now, Philip feared, the missionary activities would take a more aggressive course if formally endorsed by the Plymouth government.

Thus, to King Philip and many Wampanoags, the Sassamon decision, which had justified Plymouth's aggressive imposition of the English system upon them, was not just another blow, but the final blow. It outraged King Philip and his men and served as a rallying point. The Sassamon case, which sparked King Philip's War, was not merely a triggering incident but a legal manifestation of the primary cause of the war, the final culmination of not only legal conflict but more general confrontation between the colonists and the natives in southern New England.

Within a few days after the hangings of the two men, the Wampanoags were reported arming around Plymouth. On June 19, Philip's men attacked the colonists' frontier village of Swansea at the entrance of the Mount Hope peninsula, looting and plundering a number of the English houses, which had already been deserted, and setting them on fire. Although first blood was drawn by the English, who shot pilfering Indians in an abandoned house, the Wampanoags on June 24 killed nine men and mortally wounded two others. By June 29, when Swansea was nearly destroyed—although its Miles Garrison house withstood, being defended by the Plymouth and Massachusetts troops—King Philip's War, the "most dangerous and deadly conflict in all New England history," was on.

But the war came prematurely and in a haphazard way; the attack did indeed take Philip aback as well as surprise the English. It was hot-blooded young warriors who forced Philip to enter the war. When they attacked Swansea, did these Wampanoags think they were starting a war? Weren't they simply trying to revenge the deaths of those who had been executed by the Plymouth authorities, in accordance with the Wampanoag law of retaliation? Did Philip have any definite plan of conspiracy, when he was forced to be involved in hostilities? To what extent did Philip want to wage an all-out war with Plymouth?

Philip was seeking to maintain the autonomy of the Wampanoags and regain his independence, which would guarantee the sachem the authority to protect his people and their livelihood. To achieve such objectives, he must have had many other options than waging a war to force Plymouth colony to respect his interests. Even after the war started, Philip was ready to accept proposed impartial arbitration by the indifferent party; it was Massachusetts and Plymouth that rejected the proposal. But once having entered the war, Philip tried his best not only to build up the unity among his allies but successfully to fight against the English.

When the Wampanoags started the uprising in the early summer of 1675, they did not fight the English alone. Although the Indians of Cape Cod and the offshore islands did not join him and were able to maintain their towns intact, Philip was able to unite briefly many Indian groups from Rhode Island to Vermont and New Hampshire. The ill treatment by the English and their encroachment upon the Indian lands led King Philip, then at the head of merely five hundred Wampanoag warriors, to form a combination of all the Indians from Merrimac River to the Thames for the purpose of driving out the colonists.

Philip, who had long been trying to enroll the other New England tribes under his banner, was in the end able to secure the assistance of at least three major tribes: the Nipmucks, who had formerly been closely bound to the Wampanoags and were still under their influence, the Pocumtucks, the Nipmucks' neighboring tribe to the west, and the Narragansetts, the traditional enemies of the Wampanoags, who sided with Philip when the English declared war on them in November 1675. While King Philip was able to persuade these groups to side with him, others, especially the Nausets, the Mohegans, the Pequots, the Massachusetts, and a considerable portion of the River Tribes, refused to support Philip and sided with the English.

Philip's forces waged a successful guerrilla war against outlying settlements and farms in Plymouth at the beginning. Philip had a great ability to quickly slip away, keeping his force intact. By the end of June 1675, when the English forces invaded Mount Hope, he secretly retreated over water with the entire active force, leaving only one hundred women and children behind. Philip sojourned with Weetamoo's people in the Pocasset Country, across the Mount Hope peninsula, and succeeded in binding them to his cause. Philip's raiding parties attacked the English settlements on the frontier. Since the attack at Swansea, they had raided Rehoboth and Taunton, and, on July 9, the small town of Middleborough, where most of the houses were burned down, forcing the residents soon to abandon them.

When the combined army of Massachusetts and Plymouth moved toward the Pocasset swamp country, Philip and Weetamoo and their followers had escaped from the swamp, crossed the Taunton River, and headed northward toward the Nipmuck country. When they came to a place called Nipsachuck, some twelve miles northwest of Providence, they decided to make camp. On the early morning of August 1, the English force attacked the Wampanoags and took them by surprise. After a sharp skirmish, the Wampanoags took refuge in a swamp and hid there for the rest of the day. By the time the English forces resumed the attack with fresh reinforcements, the Wampanoags had made a clear escape. This has been regarded as the biggest blunder of the war, because if the English had destroyed the Wampanoags here, it would have ended the war.

The failure of the English at Nipsachuck caused, instead, the spread of war from the western Plymouth colony into the Nipmuck country. While Weetamoo and her people moved southward and joined the Narragansetts, Philip and his warriors moved northward to join the Nipmucks, boosting their morale.

The Nipmucks, who had had a close bond with the Wampanoags, were the first group to throw their lot in with Philip. On June 21, one day after the Wampanoags attacked Swansea, Governor Josiah Winslow of Plymouth sent a letter to Boston, urging the Massachusetts government to use its influence to keep the Nipmucks and Narragansetts from joining Philip. Winslow believed that they were just about ready to take the Wampanoag side.

The Bay Colony full-heartedly accepted Winslow's urgent request and promised to send not only two separate missions to them to prevent a possible general Indian war but also a third mission to mediate between Plymouth colony and Philip himself. A party was sent from Boston to the Nipmuck country to secure a promise of fidelity from the sachems. Most of the Nipmuck sachems denied that any of their men had gone to fight for Philip, while others promised to recall those who had gone. But the safety of the Massachusetts frontier towns was precarious.

The war, which was so far confined to the western reaches of Plymouth colony, now began to spread to the Nipmuck country. And also there was a growing suspicion that the Narragansetts were actually much more deeply involved in Philip's uprising than would appear by their statement and promises. The sachems were not abiding by their promises to surrender enemy Indians.

By early July, the war led to the division of the Nipmucks into the prowar and antiwar parties. The former, led by the sachem Muttaump, was increasingly gaining momentum and came to be supported by the majority of the Indians, especially the hotheaded young men. Ephraim Curtis, a trader who owned a trading post in the Nipmuck country, was sent by the Massachusetts government to obtain firm guarantees of fidelity from the Nipmuck sachems. When he was delivering his message of peace, on July 14, a group of Nipmuck warriors, led by the sachem Matoonas, suddenly attacked Mendon, a small frontier town in southern Massachusetts, killing several settlers.

The government of Massachusetts, however, made a last-ditch effort to secure the Nipmucks' allegiance: in late July it sent Captain Edward Hutchinson, who had just returned from his treaty-making mission to the Narragansetts, to the Nipmuck country. He set out with Curtis, three friendly Indians as guides and interpreters, and some twenty troops under the command of Captain Thomas Wheeler to meet with the Nipmuck sachems on August 2. But by then the Nipmucks, who had been inspired by the arrival of Philip and his men in the Nipmuck country the previous day, turned very belligerent. Instead of meeting Hutchinson and his party at the designated site, the Nipmucks ambushed them. The party narrowly escaped, leaving behind eight men dead or wounded on the ground. They retreated to the frontier town of Brookfield, where they secured one of the main houses as a garrison and, together with eighty residents, decided to defend themselves against impending attack.

The Nipmuck warriors maintained their tight siege of the garrison house for almost forty-eight hours, until Major Simon Willard rushed to the scene from Lancaster to rescue the colonists. Hutchinson and Wheeler, who had been wounded in the initial ambush, were taken to Marlborough, where Hutchinson died. Brookfield was defended by Willard for another several weeks but was finally abandoned.

When the war started, the experiment for Christianization of the Nipmucks abruptly ended. The critics of Praying Indians found enough excuse to expel Nipmuck Indians from the seven new Christian towns. These towns soon came to be totally abandoned, and all the Praying Indians scattered. Many of these Christian Indians located along the outer fringe of English settlements were blood-related to the more hostile Indians of the interior, and the colonists believed that most of the Praying Indians joined Philip against the English. Actually they simply withdrew to a safe distance from colonial wrath against all Indians, and after the war they settled at the missionary town of Schaghticoke in New York.

King Philip's whereabouts in August were not entirely clear, but he was suspected to have gone first to Quabaug Old Fort

(Ashquoash), a favorite Nipmuck gathering place near Brookfield, and then to Menameset, the main camp of the Nipmucks. Encouraged by the presence of Philip and the Wampanoags in their country, the Nipmucks were now extending the range of their operations. On August 22, they attacked Lancaster, killing seven of its inhabitants.

The Nipmuck force was also believed to be hovering somewhere east of the Connecticut River, between Hadley and Squakeag (Northfield), in the vicinity of Paquoag, some twenty miles northwest of Mount Wachusett. The combined forces of Massachusetts and Connecticut, together with a considerable number of Mohegan Indians, were searching for their enemies in the region.

The residents of the remote frontier towns of Deerfield and Squakeag, though they were in the middle of enemy territory, were reluctant to abandon their homes and clung to their settlements. At the beginning of September, when the Nipmucks attacked Deerfield, killing a man and burning several dwelling houses, and murdered eight others in the woods near Squakeag, it was decided that these frontier settlements were no longer safe and should be abandoned. Captain Richard Beers and his company of thirty-six men were sent to evacuate the settlements, but they were ambushed just two miles from Squakeag, where Beers and more than half of his men were killed.

For nearly four months after Philip had escaped from his home base, Mount Hope, the New England colonies had suffered a series of setbacks. It had been long suspected that the Nipmucks could not have conducted such successful campaigns against the English in the upper Connecticut Valley without Narragansett warriors secretly participating in the fighting. The speed with which the Narragansetts received news of the Nipmucks's successful attacks and the pleasure they expressed at such news demonstrated that there was close contact between them. The English declaration of war on the Narragansetts on November 12 only made the connection official and open.

When King Philip's War started, the Narragansetts did not openly enter the war but remained officially neutral. Just after the outbreak, the English urged the Narragansett sachems to prevent their men from joining the fight, but Pessacus complained that his influence over his people was being supplanted by the aggressive leadership of young men, most of whom were clamoring for war against the English.

The colonists, therefore, became very apprehensive over the role the Narragansetts might play in the war. Evidence of their hostility was mounting. Philip had long been communicating with the Narragansetts, trying to win their support. Some Narragansett warriors were reported to have participated even in the Wampanoags' initial attacks on Plymouth towns. In early July, some hot-blooded young Narragansetts plundered even their old friend Roger Williams's town, Providence. Wampanoag women and children are said to have been sheltered in the Narragansett country.

As hostilities between Philip and the English started, the Narragansett confederation began to reunite around the principal sachem Canonchet (Nananawtunu), Miantonomo's youngest son, who was born shortly before his father's execution in 1643. Pomham, a Shawomet sachem, who allied himself briefly with the Bay Colony in 1643 in an attempt to break away from Miantonomo, who pressured him to sell his land to Samuel Gorton, now became one of the ablest Narragansett soldiers.

As early as the spring of 1675, Canonchet defied the order of the United Colonies to surrender the Wampanoag refugees who participated in the initial skirmishes that led to King Philip's War and fled to the Narragansett country. "No, not a Wampanoag," declared the sachem, "nor the paring of a Wampanoag nail." But the Narragansetts were reluctant to make the final break with the English. Captain Hutchinson led an army of Massachusetts troops to Wickford, Rhode Island, where he negotiated a treaty with the Narragansetts on July 5, 1675, with the help of Roger Williams.

The treaty, however, was signed by only four subordinate counselors of the sachems, who were coerced into doing it, because Hutchinson and other officers could not persuade the real leaders to sign it. The treaty, lacking the legitimate sachems' signatures, stipulated that the Narragansetts remain loyal to the English, treat all the Wampanoags as enemies, and surrender any Wampanoag refugees in the Narragansett country. The treaty also promised the Narragansetts bounties for Wampanoags and their heads and confirmed all previous Narragansett land grants to the English. Later, the sachems of the Narragansetts and Eastern Niantics were requested to come to Boston to negotiate another treaty. The treaty of October 8, signed by Canonchet, representing the Narragansetts, and Cornman, representing Ninigret, contained nothing new except for setting the definite date for delivery of the enemy refugees. The delivery day (October 28) came and went without a single Wampanoag prisoner being turned over.

The commissioners of the United Colonies for some days contemplated making a formal declaration of war on the Narragansetts, but finally on November 12 they did make the decision. The colonists' war with the Narragansetts had been intended as a "preventive war," but the question still remains as to whether the Narragansetts would definitely have joined Philip without the English first declaring war on them. On Sunday, December 19, the army of the United Colonies attacked and destroyed the Narragansett palisaded fort in the Great Swamp (southwest of Kingston), killing over two hundred warriors, in addition to numerous women and children who died in the burning wigwams. All told, nearly one thousand were either killed or captured. The remaining Narragansetts were forced to go into guerrilla exile. After that the Narragansetts fought not only against the colonial armies who invaded their land but in the territories of the Nipmucks and other allied groups.

By December, Philip, who had been in the Nipmuck country since August, journeyed with some of his forces to the Mahican Indians north of Albany in order to secure their support and alliance. At the request of the Puritan colonies, the New York governor, Edmund Andros, pressured the fierce Mohawks to attack Philip and his men. Instead of supporting them, the Mohawks killed some and put the rest to flight. It happened once again. As in the Pequot War, the Mohawks, who were motivated by self-interest, sought to enhance their own power by playing powerful intermediaries between the English and the Indians, and they fought against enemies of the English in the New England backcountry. This was a serious setback for Philip; he not only failed to obtain the powerful Mohawks' support but incurred losses at their hands. Disappointed, Philip and his forces returned to the Nipmuck country.

During the early months of 1676, the Nipmucks were most active in the vicinity of Menameset on the Ware River, Washaccum, and Mount Wachusett. On February 10, the Nipmucks attacked Lancaster and took away Mrs. Mary Rowlandson, wife of the town's minister, and children and other relatives, when the minister had gone to Boston. The next victim was Medfield, a settlement less than twenty miles southwest of Boston that was raided at daybreak on February 21 by several hundred Nipmucks, who burned nearly fifty houses and barns. Then they withdrew, taking the bridge over the Charles River to Sherborn, and then set the bridge on fire to prevent pursuit, "hurling taunts and insults at the settlers," who were standing helplessly on the other side of the river. As they withdrew, the Nipmucks tacked to a tree a note (probably written by James Printer), which read as follows:

> Know by this paper, that the Indians that thou hast provoked to wrath and anger, will war this twenty one years if you will; there are many Indians yet, we come three hundred at this time. You must consider the Indians lose nothing but their life; you must lose your fair houses and cattle & much good things.

Four days later, the Nipmucks reached near the very coast of Massachusetts, when they attacked Weymouth, setting fire to a number of buildings.

From late February on, the Nipmucks began to concentrate their activities along the Massachusetts frontier towns east of Mount Wachusett. The major attack came on March 13, when the Nipmucks, led by a prominent sachem, Monoco (One-Eyed John, Apequinash), raided Groton and burned the meeting house and a large number of dwellings; but the garrison houses, where most of the residents had stayed, successfully withstood the assault. The Groton people, however, soon abandoned the town and took refuge at Concord.

By the end of March, the tide began to turn slowly to the English side, as the Nipmucks seemed rapidly to be losing their momentum and resources. Massachusetts had begun by negotiating with the Nipmucks clustered around Mount Wachusett. Although peace was the long-range objective of its negotiations, the Bay Colony's immediate goal was the recovery of English captives. For the release of Mrs. Rowlandson the Nipmucks first demanded a twenty-pound ransom, but after much haggling, the Massachusetts delegates were able to obtain her release without a ransom. The proposed meeting for peace never took place, because the Indians were simply gaining time and were not serious about concluding the war. Redeemed or escaped captives, however, began to appear at various towns during the spring and early summer.

The situation of the Nipmucks as well as those of other pro-Philip groups worsened in late spring. Sharp divisions developed among themselves: the older and more prudent Indians advocated negotiations for peace, while the younger and more ardent warriors opposed any talks. The shortage of food, which they had been experiencing since winter, became more acute. As the Indians endeavored to secure new sources of food supply, fishing at the river falls and planting crops at remote places, Indian military activities began to slow down.

The spring of 1676 was also a critical period for the Narragansetts. In March, a Narragansett force of four hundred under Canonchet devastated Captain Michael Pierce's company of sixty-three soldiers and twenty Cape Cod Indians near the Blackstone River (Central Falls, Rhode Island), killing fifty-two English and eleven Nausets. In April, however, Canonchet was captured by a combined force (forty-seven Connecticut militia and Mohegan and Pequot Indians) at Seaconk near the Pawtuxet River, when he had come down into his native country to obtain seed corn.

{ *Igniting King Philip's War* }

Canonchet was told that his life would be spared if he agreed to live in peace with the English, but the thirty-three-year-old sachem found the conditions utterly unacceptable and opted to face death with dignity. He is reported to have said, "I shall die before my heart is soft; before I have said anything unworthy of Canonchet to say." The English allowed Oweneco, Uncas's son, and his Mohegan firing squad to execute Canonchet at Stonington near the west bank of the Pawcatuck River, thus perpetuating the continuing Narragansett-Mohegan enmity. His body was mutilated by the Mohegans and cremated by the Eastern Niantics in a fire kindled by the warriors under Catapazat, son of the Pequot chief, Harmon Garrett. Canonchet's head was sent on to the council at Hartford as evidence of the victory.

Canonchet, tall and strongly built, was a sturdy young warrior-sachem with a proud fighting spirit and was a relentless foe of the English. Some colonists naturally condemned him as a "damned wretch" and a "monster of cruelty," but Canonchet, nevertheless, earned the high respect of the native people, friends and foes alike. He was a man of courage and ability, and his fame at times was hardly less than that of King Philip.

Why did the Narragansetts, who had been a traditional enemy of the Wampanoags for a long time, take the side of the Wampanoags and decide to cast in their lot with them? To be sure, there had been a close kinship relation between the two groups, including Philip's sister-in-law Weetamoo, who had married the Narragansett sachem Quinnapin. But the main reason why the Narragansetts became the Wampanoags' strongest ally, fighting the war to the end, sharing their fate, willing to go down with them, was the Narragansetts' firm adherence to their independence and autonomy and their willingness to fight to maintain it, a conviction they fully shared with the Wampanoags.

After the death of Canonchet, however, the Narragansett power was effectively broken, a situation reminiscent of the Narragansetts in the early 1640s, when his father was assassinated. Many of the survivors were forced to abandon their country and fled to the North and the South. Pessacus, who was a reluctant enemy of the English and an advocate of peace, took a small band of followers and fled north, but he was killed by hostile Mohawks in an ambush near Piscataqua. Others found refuge with the Niantics, who, under the sachem Ninigret, had refused to take part in the war.

Quaiapen, the sister of Ninigret, who had married Canonicus's son Mixanno and fully participated in the Narragansett political decisions, played a responsible leadership role in the war, but she was slain in July 1676 when Major John Talcott's troops attacked Nipsachuck Swamp in North Smithfield, killing or taking prisoner 171 Narragansetts, including women and children. After the war, many of the defeated Narragansetts fled to the Eastern Niantics, with whom many of Pessacus's men had already sought refuge during the war, while other survivors submitted to long periods of indentureship to various colonial families.

Meanwhile, Philip, together with considerable numbers of Wampanoags and some Narragansetts, had returned by July 1676 from the Nipmuck country to the southwestern reaches of Plymouth Colony. As the tide began to turn, Philip, who had lost all the options available to him, returned to Mount Hope to die, driven "by some great compelling sense of tragic drama." Captain Benjamin Church of Plymouth and his men were now closing in on the returning Wampanoags in their native land. They killed Philip's uncle, Akkompoin, and captured some Indians, among whom they found Philip's wife, Wootonekanuske, and his nine-year-old-son, but Philip himself managed to evade capture. The remnants of Philip's forces, which were no longer capable of any organized resistance, now became mere wandering fugitives fleeing before the English. In early August, Church's men captured two dozen Wampanoags under the Pocasset squaw sachem Weetamoo, wife of the Narragansett sachem Quinnapin. Weetamoo successfully escaped, but drowned while crossing the Taunton River to get to her own country.

Finally, on August 12, 1676, Philip and a small group of companions were tracked down in his old headquarters at Mount Hope, and Philip was killed by one of the Indian allies of the English. Captain Church, who described the dead Philip as looking like only "a doleful, great, naked, dirty beast," ordered the body decapitated and quartered. Philip's head was taken to Plymouth, where it is said to have been exposed on a pole in the town square for twenty years.

One of the last to hold out after Philip's death was his brother-in-law and Sassamon's father-in-law, Tuspaquin, sachem of Assawompsett. He was at the head of the large party of Indians who, in the spring of 1676, hung about the towns in Plymouth and made successful raids against Scituate, Bridgewater, and Plymouth. When the wandering bands were reduced to a few handfuls, he and his family were captured. Captain Church promised him that their lives should be spared. When he was taken to Plymouth, Church was not there to defend him. Tuspaquin was immediately tried and executed.

Philip's ablest lieutenant, Annawon, escaped but was later captured by Church, who spent one of the most unusual nights of his life with Annawon at his camp, being treated courteously, hospitably, and generously. Annawon presented Church, as a token of submission, several beautiful bead belts and other regalia once belonging to Philip. Church was deeply impressed by Annawon's nobility and dignity, took a real liking to this most distinguished prisoner, and hoped that his life would be spared, but Annawon was taken to Plymouth, where he was subsequently executed at the same time as Tuspaquin.

In King Philip's War, the most destructive in the history of New England, the Wampanoags were practically exterminated, and the survivors fled to the interior tribes. Male captives believed to have actively fought against the English were executed, and many of those who were captured, including Philip's wife and little boy, were sold into slavery in the West Indies, while others joined the various praying towns in Massachusetts. The greater part of the Wampanoags who remained in the country joined their affiliate, the Sakonnets.

As Philip and his followers left the Nipmuck country for their home land, Shoshanim (known as Sagamore Sam) and some other Nipmuck sachems in early July began a new correspondence with the Massachusetts government, trying to exonerate themselves. But the authorities insisted that mercy would not be extended to those who started the war or engaged in atrocities, and also made it clear that they would not discuss peace until all the English captives were released. Then came the news of a possible Mohawk attack against the New England Indians, causing great consternation among the Nipmucks and other pro-Philip Indians. The Connecticut authorities at Hartford, who did not want the fierce Mohawks marauding within the colony, suggested that instead of the Connecticut Indians they attack the Nipmucks in the Squakeag and Mount Wachusett areas. But the Mohawk invasion never took place.

More and more, disillusioned Nipmucks voluntarily stopped fighting in the hope of saving their lives. Some merely presented themselves at an English settlement, while others took refuge with other native communities that had remained loyal to the English. Uncas, above all, became a possible savior to these Nipmucks.

On July 27, Monoco, who launched the major attack on Groton in March but confessed that he did not kill a single colonist, led about 180 of his people to Boston to hand them over to the Massachusetts authorities. Monoco brought with him, as a further sign of his submission, securely bound with rope, the much sought after sachem Matoonas and his son, whom Monoco and his men tricked and captured as the ransom for their own lives. The colonial authorities took Matoonas immediately to Boston Common, tied him to a tree, had him shot to death by Monoco and his men, and placed his head on a pole for display.

The Eastern Niantics, although they had been close allies of the Narragansetts since the early 1640s, acted independently during King Philip's War and maintained a nominal pro-English position and abstained from personal activity. They had trouble, however, in keeping on terms with the English. In the September 1675 conference held at Wickford between the Narragansetts/ Niantics and the English regarding the surrender of the Wampanoag fugitives, Ninigret was the only sachem who firmly adhered to the agreement of July 15, thus seriously jeopardizing the unity of the Narragansett confederation.

By the end of October, when it was reported that Canonchet

was planning to attack the English in the spring, only Ninigret and the Niantics steadfastly promised continued support to the English. Yet a number of the Niantics are rumored to have fought against the English in the Great Swamp fight.

Although the Niantics since early 1676 supported the English, serving in the Indian auxiliaries of the United Colonies armies and of the Connecticut army that conducted independent operations in the Narragansett country, they did not get along well with the other two English allies: the Mohegans and the Pequots. The triangular rivalry among them became more intense as time progressed, when the opportunity for plunder became greater, seriously hurting English war efforts and objectives.

The United Colonies, which well recognized the critical position held by Ninigret during the war, were for a time entertaining the idea of utilizing Ninigret's good offices for a speedy conclusion of the war. The Eastern Niantics emerged intact from the war. They, in fact, were one of the few Indian groups that did not take part in the fighting against the English and thus escaped the disruption, relocation, and severe loss of life experienced by those groups that took on Philip's cause. After the war the Niantics absorbed many of the Narragansett survivors, but the entire group, the combined but mainly Niantic population, came to be called henceforth the Narragansetts. They were assigned a tract near Charlestown, Rhode Island.

Ninigret, "an old crafty sachem," as Increase Mather called him, died full of years in 1679. He, like many other sachems in southern New England, steadfastly opposed Christianity and told the missionary Matthew Mayhew to "go and make the English good first." Ninigret's daughter, Weunquesh, served as sachem until her death in 1686, when she was succeeded by a series of male sachems. In 1709, Ninigret II, son of the deceased sachem, quitclaimed all the title to vacant Narragansett (Niantic) lands to Rhode Island, except for a tract of some sixty-four square miles in Charlestown for him and his people, to be kept perpetually. Although the Rhode Island legislature exercised control over the tribe from without, the sachem and an appointed five-man council governed from within.

The Pequots, who had received harsh treatment from the English some forty years earlier, participated in the war on the English side almost from the beginning. It was simply a matter of policy that they join the English, for their enemies were on the other side. They served as part of the Indian auxiliary troops for Connecticut, which made the most extensive and efficient use of loyal Indian troops. In the July campaign of 1675, the Pequots served under Captain Wait Winthrop, and in the Great Swamp fight on December 17, Major Robert Treat of Connecticut had, besides the English army of over three hundred, about three hundred Pequots and Mohegans led by the Pequot Catapazat and Uncas's oldest son, Oweneco. It was a speedy Pequot who pursued the Narragansett sachem Canonchet and captured him in April 1676.

After the war, the two Pequot communities, the Mashantucket and the Paucatuck, remained intact. Gradually, however, closer and tighter supervision of the Connecticut government over them and the corresponding decline of their autonomous power were making the Pequot communities more like reservations.

The Mohegans were another group that fought for the English. Uncas, after all he had done for the English over the years, was not yet fully trusted. Some definitely feared that he would take Philip's side. At the outbreak of the war, the English ordered Uncas to come to Boston. He complied, sent six delegates, and offered immediate aid to the English. The English demand for hostages as an assurance of Uncas's sincerity was accepted by him, and he arranged to send his son Oweneco's wife and child to Hartford. The Mohegans remained allied with the English throughout the war and fought against the Wampanoags, Narragansetts, and Nipmucks, serving as an Indian auxiliary force to the colonial army, usually under Oweneco. The Mohegans were able to retain their land, guns, and autonomy, and, quite different from the Indian groups that sided with Philip, they avoided the suffering of the invasion by English troops, defeat, enslavement, and dispersion.

Toward the end of the war, Uncas as a powerful chieftain was viewed as a possible savior by many pro-Philip Indians, and Mohegan villages in eastern Connecticut became a mecca for those frightened fugitives. Uncas apparently welcomed these refugees in the hope that he could absorb them and increase his strength. Their presence in the Mohegan villages, however, became a source of great concern to the neighboring English settlers.

By the end of the war, the Mohegans, as one of the few Indian groups siding with the victor, were the only important group remaining in southern New England, but not for long. The destruction of the enemies of the Mohegans, such as the Wampanoags, Narragansetts, and Nipmucks, simply did not help the Mohegans, but caused their decline. The elimination of the major Indian powers ended the colonists' necessity to support and protect the Mohegans. On the other hand, the Mohegans by then had exhausted lands to sell and give as a means to receive favor from the colonial government. Within a decade, it became clear that the Mohegans' situation was not much better than that of natives who had lost the war. As aging Uncas fell into obscurity and as the English settlement expanded, the Mohegans sold most of their lands and confined themselves to a reservation on the Thames River in the New London area.

They became more and more dependent upon the Connecticut government for their livelihood. Uncas and the subsequent sachems filed numerous petitions with the General Court, asking for its action on a variety of matters: exclusion of other Indians from hunting on the Mohegan land, damages caused by the settlers' cattle on their land, more suitable land for cultivation, the right to hunt, fish, and gather on the land they had already alienated, boundary disputes with neighboring English towns, and grants-in-aid to alleviate desperate living conditions. The Mohegan population declined to 750 by 1705, and was further reduced to 206 by 1774.

Other southern New England Indian groups participated in King Philip's War on their own as friends and foes of the Wampanoags. Most of the Massachusetts Indians supported the English cause, but some of them who had close ties of kinship with Wampanoags, or other groups friendly to them, took Philip's side. For example, James the Printer, a Natick Indian, who had assisted Sergeant Green and Marmaduke Johnson in printing the Indian Bible in Cambridge, led a Nipmuck marauding party against the English. He later served as scribe for the Nipmuck sachems in the negotiations for the release of Mrs. Rowlandson, who was held as a captive by the tribe. Toward the end of the war, responding to the Massachusetts special declaration of mercy issued on June 19, 1676, James and some others came into Cambridge and made a penitent surrender.

The overwhelming majority of the Praying Indians, however, chose the English side. Within a month, fifty-two Massachusetts Indians took part in a campaign against Philip's stronghold at Mount Hope, a contribution the English commander highly praised. Especially valuable were their services as guides, scouts, spies, and informants. Two Christian Indians, James Quannapohit and Job Kattenanit, who were sent deep into the Nipmuck country in central Massachusetts as spies, brought back much useful information for the English.

The majority of the Praying Indians took little active part in the war, but they suffered greatly from the anti-Indian hysteria among the colonists. The initial successes of the Indian enemy in the first few months and examples of their deliberate treachery caused the English to become suspicious of all Indians, including those who had long been peaceful and friendly. The Praying Indians became the targets of unreasonable search, illegal arrest, irresponsible shooting, and other rough treatment by the English.

Finally, in October 1675, the General Court decided to intern Natick Indians on Deer Island in Boston Harbor, not only to prevent them from aiding the enemy but to protect them from the blind anger of the English. The confinement the Indians endured on the island for seven months until May 1676 was dreadful. They suffered from lack of adequate clothing and shelter and, especially, a serious shortage of food supply, forcing them to live virtually on clams and other shellfish they could find on the shore at low tide. At one time a group of men from Lynn plotted to invade Deer Island and slaughter all the natives on the island, among whom, ironically, many valuable Indian guides, spies, and scouts, like Kattenanit and Quannapohit, were recruited. Only the timely discovery of the plot prevented a possible disaster. To the Naticks, other Praying Indians from Nashobah and Punkapaug were added, making the total native population on the island five hundred.

The friendly Indians came deeply to resent the colonists' vindictiveness and became so afraid of their English neighbors that some of them fled to the hostile tribes, while others went beyond the reach of warring peoples. In November 1675, for example, when Hassanemesit Praying Village was attacked by the hostile Indians, some two hundred men, women, and children were taken away, many of them leaving willingly. These Hassanemesits, who had already been disarmed by the English, were convinced that the unfriendly English neighbors, who had been abusing and threatening them, would destroy them if they stayed.

The fourteen praying towns John Eliot and other missionaries established before the war, the seven original towns among the Massachusetts and seven new towns among the Nipmucks (four in Massachusetts and three in Connecticut), underwent a drastic transformation. During the war, all Christian Indians were compelled to live in one of five towns: Natick, Punkapaug, Nashobah, Wamesit, and Hassanemesit. The end of the war did not improve the condition of these Indians. In May 1677, the Praying Indians, as well as other Indians in the Bay colony, were ordered to be confined to one of the four towns of Natick, Punkapaug (Staughton), Hassanemesit (Grafton), and Wamesit (Chelmsford), with the exception of Indian children and servants living within the English communities. Four years later, the number of the Indian towns where the Indians were required to live was reduced to three, Natick, Punkapaug, and Wamesit. Moreover, these towns, drastically reduced in number, were now transformed into reservations and came to be administered more closely and strictly by the colonial government.

One of the three major allies of the Wampanoags, the Pocumtucks, who lived on the upper Connecticut River, supported Philip, as did the Nipmucks to the east, but did not substantially contribute because their war with the Mohawks in the 1660s had already exhausted them. They joined with bands of Nipmucks and Narragansetts, raiding Hadley, Northampton, Deerfield, Springfield, and other colonial frontier towns. Other minor groups, like the Nonotuks in the Northampton region and the Agawans in the Springfield area, also supported King Philip and joined with the Nipmuck and Narragansett bands, raiding many English towns. They, like all other groups that sided with the Wampanoags, suffered heavy losses in 1676. Many of the survivors fled to New York and Canada. Some of the Pocumtucks remained in Scaticook on the Hudson until about 1754, when they joined the Indians in the French interest at St. Francis, Quebec. The Poquonnocs and some other "River Indians," who sided with the Wampanoags, went off with the pro-Philip Indians at the end of the war, never to return to their native land. Most of them (such as the Podunks, the Wongunks, and the Siciaoggs), however, supported the English but did not take part actively in the fighting.

The Pennacooks, the southernmost tribe of the northern New England Indians, continued to maintain their traditional policy of peace and friendship with the English during King Philip's War. When the war started, the sachem Wannalancet had no desire to be dragged into it and withdrew his people northward to avoid the war, a move that only aroused the suspicions of the English. Captain Samuel Moseley, known for his rough-handedness, led his men deep into Pennacook country in September and burned an Indian village, but the sachem still refused to strike back.

The Bay Colony authorities were appalled by Moseley's unprovoked assault and tried to remedy the situation. Efforts were made to meet with Wannalancet to persuade him and his people to come to live at Wamesit, or at least to renew articles of peace to restore friendly relations. All efforts, however, failed; Wannalancet had been long gone and had disappeared into the northern wilderness, where the peace his people desired would be fully guaranteed.

In early June 1676, Wannalancet, accompanied by some other Indians and several English captives, came to Dover, New Hampshire, in order to reestablish his former good relationship with the

English. On July 3, a treaty of peace and amity was signed by Wannalancet, representing the Indians, and Major Richard Waldron of Dover, for the English. It pledged the fidelity of a large number of Indians living in the area between the Merrimac and Kennebec rivers. Most of the Pennacooks, however, went to Canada, and in 1677 they tried to persuade Wannalancet to come and settle with them, but he declined the offer and returned eventually to the Merrimac.

Just as it started, King Philip's War, which embroiled all peoples in southern New England—both the English and the Indians—for fourteen months, slowly and gradually smoldered down. This war, which put the finishing touches on the organized Indian resistance in the region, resembled in many ways the Pequot War, which had taken place forty years earlier.

These wars were both essentially conflicts between the English and the Indians. Some of the Indian groups, to be sure, sided with the English colonists, but no colonists ever took the side of the Indians in either war, though some English did oppose the conflicts. These wars were both contests for dominance and challenges to the opposing cultural, legal, and economic systems.

For the Indians, the objectives of the wars were different. In the Pequot War, the main issue among the Indian groups was the preservation of their self-interest. They formed alliances with each other and with the English in order to protect and advance their own political, economic, and cultural interests. By King Philip's War, however, it was more fundamental, more than just self-interest. Their main concern was their very survival as independent and autonomous entities, in which they could perpetuate their traditional way of life and livelihood. But only a small number of Indian groups determined to protect such rights, such as the Wampanoags, Narragansetts, and Nipmucks, fought against the English. Those who fought on the English side, like the Mohegans, were no longer independent nations, but heavily dependent upon the English. Their aspiration for autonomy and self-determination had long gone, and those goals were no longer their concern.

The destruction in the Pequot War, especially at Fort Mystic, not only shocked the Indians, the Pequot enemies and the English allies alike, but also surprised the English. New England Indians had not been used to killing men, women, and children indiscriminately. Although many contemporary English colonists and later historians have justified what the English soldiers did, some continue to criticize severely the English actions in the war.

The author of the most recent, definitive history of the war insists that the "deliberate, cold-blooded slaughters of women and children as well as warriors" in the burning of Fort Mystic cannot be dismissed as "a military necessity." "The massacre at Fort Mystic," he concludes, "was an act of terrorism intended to break Pequot morale." This is certainly a convincing statement for those who view the war from peacetime and retrospectively.

The early American settlers, both military men and civilians, however, did not have the benefit of hindsight. Some justified the English actions, insisting that the attack at Mystic was a retribution, though harsh and excessive, for the small number of the English killed at the beginning at Gardener's Saybock fort and at Wethersfield. Others argued that the English, with a small population and tiny settlements, were in a very precarious situation in the latter part of the 1630s. Overestimating the number and strength of the Pequot enemies in a vast country unfamiliar to them, the colonists were willing to use any ruthless tactics to win the war.

Such daring English commanders as Mason, Underhill, and Gardener, who came from the long military tradition of Europe, must have been familiar with the military secret of the Mongolians, who had established the vast Eurasian empire in the thirteenth century. Masters of espionage and psychological warfare, the Mongols put "whole cities to the sword," butchering "to a man" and raping, slaughtering, and enslaving "their women and children." The Mongols, "inhuman monsters," as the Europeans called them, let "such terrors run ahead of them as a weapon in itself," and made sure nothing could stand against them. Genghis Khan's name had thus been mentioned "with fear and awe throughout the civilized world," even before he died.

{ *Igniting King Philip's War* }

The story of Mongolian conquest had, therefore, been told repeatedly among the Europeans and still remained fresh and vivid in the minds of the early-seventeenth-century Europeans, especially military men, including those who came to the New World. The Europeans would not dare employ such Mongolian tactics among themselves, in Europe or America, but they were willing to put them into practice fighting against the "infidels" in North America.

Regardless of the moral aspect of the Pequot War, both the Indians and the English learned valuable lessons from it. The Indians quickly adjusted themselves to English warfare, adopted their strategies and weapons, and fought like the English fighters, or even more efficiently, in the next war. Using the unique topography they were so well familiar with, especially effective use of trackless swamps, into which they retreated whenever necessary, they resorted to guerrilla warfare with surprise attacks, ambushes, and indiscriminate destruction of English villages, without sparing women and children.

The Indians also came to learn the use of English weapons. Thus King Philip's War turned out to be no longer a contest between "flintlock and tomahawk," because the Indians by then could use flintlocks as effectively as the English did.

In the Pequot War, the English commanders such as Mason and Underhill witnessed their Indian allies' moderation, reluctance, and tameness in fighting and became very disgusted with them. During King Philip's War, however, the English military leaders quickly learned effective use of friendly Indians, who turned out to be very skillful in tracking and forest maneuvers. By contrast, the English soldiers had been ruthless but effective and daring fighters in the Pequot War, but the English armies in King Philip's War, probably because of their underestimation of the Indian fighting ability (an underestimation developed in their minds for the last forty years), did not fight an effective war. Their ineptitude and lack of decisiveness and the daring attacks caused the English to miss many chances for a speedy conclusion of the war.

Conclusion: The World Upside Down

The Sassamon case and King Philip's War that followed marked a significant turning point in Indian-English relations in southern New England. The victory in the war, though they paid dearly for it, provided the English colonists the opportunity not only to vindicate their legal action taken in the Sassamon case but to promote the expansion of English settlements at the expense of the Indian tribal system. Now the colonists were able to take over the Indian land, confining the Indians to small areas and forcing them at the same time to conform to the colonial way.

For the Wampanoags and their allies, war and defeat meant destruction, hardship, suffering, and more suffering. Many warriors were either killed in the war or executed, and the survivors—soldiers, women, and children alike—were sold into slavery, drastically reducing their already weak population. The rest of the survivors were forced to live under foreign and unfriendly conditions, dictated by the colonists, that totally ignored their traditional way of life.

Those Indians who sided with the English, unfortunately, met virtually the same fate. Their land was continually being taken away by the English through purchase, if not by confiscation, and their village system rapidly reduced to nil. The Indians, both victors' allies and defeated, had to live the life dictated by the victors, and there was, in a few decades, no distinction between them.

From the legal perspective, the Sassamon case set a new era. The fact that this case, which involved only Indians but was decided by the English, came to be justified by the winning of the war, made the principles embodied in the case the prevailing legal basis. The Sassamon case stands, therefore, at a crucial point in the transition from legal coexistence to legal imperialism.

During the pre–King Philip's War era, the Wampanoags and the Plymouth colony lived in uneasy accommodation, but most of the intercultural disputes were settled based upon the assumption that the colony and the Indian group were two independent political entities. Increasingly in the early 1670s, the colonists began to modify their policies and assert their legal jurisdiction over the Indians. The aggressive extension of their jurisdiction and assertive policy maintained in the Sassamon murder trial and executions, which were carried out quickly and without consultation with the Indians, caused violent reactions among the Wampanoags, which in turn led directly to the war.

Just as the Southerners' assertion of state sovereignty ended in the Civil War, so Indian independence and autonomy died with King Philip's War. The war officially marked the end of legal coexistence between the English and the New England Indians and the beginning of legal imperialism, which placed all the Indians within limits of the colony under the jurisdiction of the colonial courts. The war did hasten the deterioration of the independent status of Indian bands in the entire New England area. The very small number of the surviving members of the defeated groups and some friendly Indians were forced to live in a few reservations, making independent Indian government virtually disappear from southern New England. Even those on the frontier began to lose their political independence and became more and more peoples protected by the colonial governments. The process was the same, the transition only slower and more gradual. One significant trend was the change in the gender role. After the war, the male-dominated society prevailed, and as the sachems' autonomous power declined, the authority of squaw sachems declined, and women's opportunities for political leadership considerably diminished.

From the racial perspective, the subjugation of the Indians and elimination of their independent political system meant that these detribalized natives had to live in designated villages, be placed under the strict law of the colony, and be subjected to all kinds of colonial prejudice and mistreatment as a minority group.

The Indian villages, in which most of these people went to live, were after the war turned into reservations, which colonial governments used as a means to control Indians effectively. Although the Indian village in the eighteenth century became a voluntary rather than compulsory establishment, in which the Indians had more freedom than in the late seventeenth century, the Indian reservation never became an integral part of the political system of the colony. It was outside the political divisions of the colony and thus did not attain the status of township, the basic political and territorial unit in colonial New England. There is no evidence that a reservation ever sent representatives to the colonial government.

Those Indians living in the English communities did not achieve equal status with the English settlers, but were treated increasingly as a minority cultural group, together with the blacks and poor whites. While Indians were treated almost like the English in the conventional fields of law, both procedural and substantive, the special laws that had been passed in the early seventeenth century to safeguard the Indians were all abolished by the beginning of the eighteenth century, making the Indians subject to the ordinary laws, just like the English settlers. Instead, a new set of special regulations began to control various activities of the Indians in their daily life. They were even placed under a curfew law in their own land! Nor were the Indians given the chance to become citizens.

For the New England Indians, the second half of the seventeenth century was very bleak, indeed. Yet they must have looked at the Sassamon case and King Philip's War as their final effort—desperate, futile, and belated though it was—to protect the last remnants of Indian sovereignty, about which they no doubt had no regret. They did fight bravely for the cause they believed in; in fact, the Wampanoag warriors seldom surrendered, but were only captured. Nor were many tears shed over the disaster confronting them during and after the war and the hardship the innocent women and children had to undergo.

At the end of King Philip's War, the Wampanoags and other southern New England Indians could look back for the last fifty years and see nothing but revolutionary changes. Why had the world to change so drastically in such a short time? Remarks made by some Indian leaders clearly reveal their nostalgic feeling toward their good old days. "Our fathers had plenty of deer and skins," Miantonomo reminded his fellow Indians, while Philip pointed out to a settler that when the English landed, they were "a litell Child," but they became strong because of generous land grants made by his father, "a great man."

Philip, like many other Indian chiefs, could not effectively cope with the rapidly changing world. In Mount Hope, the homeland of King Philip, his descendants believe that because he was not only unable to accomplish his goals but also denied a proper burial, Philip's ghost roams the land, and they encounter him frequently. Despite the most adverse circumstances after the war, the Indians have survived, and their tradition has persisted and lived on up to the present, which historians and ethnohistorians have been recently discovering. What the Wampanoags have done, in retrospect, would deserve the admiration of the victors.

In the history of the Wampanoags and other southern New England Indian groups, the third quarter of the seventeenth century was the most critical period. It all started with John Sassamon. Like many other Indians who grew up in two cultures, Sassamon was not fully treated with respect and trust by either society. His loyalty became divided, and, therefore, he was often accused of being disloyal by one or the other.

At the same time, through his upbringing and training, he acquired valuable skill and knowledge, by which he could provide useful service to both societies. His skill and work were absolutely essential to societies that did not consider him truly loyal and viewed him with suspicion.

The role Sassamon played as a go-between was very similar to that of "Atlantic creoles," who lived along the periphery of the Atlantic coast of Africa and were eventually transported to North America and sold as slaves. These creoles were products of mixed European-African marriages in the commercial outposts along the African coast. Like Sassamon, they served as intermediaries, but their activities were in the international trade that covered Europe, Africa, and the New World.

They used the advantages of their linguistic skills and their familiarity with diverse commercial practices in the Atlantic world. As European trade expanded, the need for the creoles' service increased, giving them a powerful bargaining position. Sassamon's position was very similar; his language skill in English and the Algonquian language put him in a position only a few people could hold, enabling him to use it to his advantage.

Like Sassamon, these creoles, as people of mixed ancestry, had an identity crisis. When they adopted African ways, Europeans declared them outcasts, while Africans rejected their Africanness when they adopted European ways, and both groups ridiculed their mixed lineage. This lack of identity with one group put creoles in a precarious situation, making them vulnerable to all kinds of dangers, such as ostracism, scapegoating, and even enslavement.

Sassamon seems to have been in a better situation than the Atlantic creoles. He was a well-respected minister of the Indian church, and at the same time he had established in-law relations with some of the Wampanoag sachems, including King Philip. He was willing to use his language skill and his close contact with the colonial leaders to deal with the Wampanoag leaders aggressively. Yet he was still in the "middling," vulnerable position, because he was not well trusted despite his indispensable skill.

Whether or not he was one of the best, most qualified, and well-trained go-betweens but failed to serve well in his diplomacy because he had to deal with two irreconcilable societies is still a matter of conjecture. But when he was found dead, each side took him as one of its own. For Plymouth, Sassamon was not only a valuable individual but evidence of their successful attempt at civilization and Christianization of the Indians. There was no question, therefore, whether he was part of Plymouth society. The colony insisted that it should take full responsibility to investigate his death, despite a strong protest from the Wampanoags, with some of whom he had strong kinship ties.

Regardless of who was responsible for it, the death of Sassamon did create enormous tension, making it a pivotal movement in the decline in peaceful relations between the colonists and the New England Indians and causing a profound impact on both societies. On a more personal basis, as Sassamon died his tragic death, everything he had been associated with started to be annihilated. In his home town, Middleborough, most of the houses were burned, destroyed, and abandoned during the early stage of the war. Many of his relatives and friends, including his father-in-law (a sachem) and his uncle-in-law (chief sachem), either died or were killed in the war or were executed after the war. Like Atlantic creoles, Sassamon was vulnerable to dangers—not to "ostracism, scapegoating, and enslavement," but to death.

1580	Massasoit (Ousamequin) is born.
cir. 1620	John Sassamon is born.
November 1620	The Pilgrims land at Plymouth.
1621	On March 22, Massasoit concludes a treaty with Plymouth (the first English-Indian treaty in New England). Nine other sachems sign similar treaties with Plymouth within a few months.
1629–1630	The Massachusetts Bay Company is formed and Salem is settled in 1629. A large number of Puritans and their followers land at Boston in 1630.
1632	John Eliot starts missionary work among the Massachusett Indians and becomes acquainted with the early teenager John Sassamon.
1632–1633	The Narragansetts try to capture Massasoit, but he flees to Plymouth for protection.
1635	First three Connecticut towns, Windsor, Hartford, and Wethersfield, are settled by people from the Massachusetts Bay colony.
1636	Roger Williams is banished from Massachusetts and settles in the Narragansett country in January. He and his followers found Providence Plantation in June.
1637	The Pequot War begins. John Sassamon serves the English under Captain John Underhill.

May 1637	The colonial forces attack the Mystic fort and kill 300 to 700 Pequot, including women and children.
1638	Treaty of Hartford formally concludes the Pequot War. The Peach trial is held, and all four Plymouth men are convicted of murdering a Narragansett man; all are executed, except one who escapes. Metacom is born.
1639	Massasoit renews his original treaty with Plymouth.
September 1643	Uncas kills Miantonomo.
April 1644	Roger Williams submits in person the Narragansetts' act of submission to the English King.
1648	Ninigret, the sachem of the Eastern Niantics, becomes virtually the head of the Narragansett and Eastern Niantic confederation.
1651	Sassamon is appointed as a schoolmaster of John Eliot's praying town in Natick.
1653–1654	Sassamon attends Harvard College.
1656	Sassamon leaves Natick, goes to the Wampanoags, and works for the sachems in various capacities.
1660	Massasoit dies at the age of 80. His oldest son, Wamsutta, succeeds him as the chief sachem of the Wampanoags. Wamsutta and Metacom change their names to Alexander

	and Philip, respectively. Sassamon becomes official secretary for Wamsutta.
1662	Alexander dies. Philip succeeds him as the chief sachem. Sassamon becomes Philip's interpreter and secretary. On August 6, at Plymouth, Philip takes the oath of loyalty to the English and also formally renews the old treaty of Massasoit.
1662–1666	Philip-Ninigret relationship starts to deteriorate.
cir. 1669	Sassamon returns to Natick.
cir. 1671	Sassamon settles at Nemasket (Middleborough) to serve as the preacher of its praying town.
1671	On September 29, Philip is forced to sign a treaty with Plymouth Colony.
1672	Governor Thomas Prence of Plymouth dies and is succeeded by Josiah Winslow.
December 1674	Sassamon meets with Philip at his hunting camp near Middleborough.
January 1675	In early January, Sassamon travels to Plymouth to warn Governor Josiah Winslow of Philip's plans of conspiracy against the English. On January 29, Sassamon is found dead at Assawompsett Pond near Middleborough.
March 1675	Three of Philip's men, Tobias, Wampapaquan, and Mattashunnamo, are indicted for the murder of Sassamon. King

Philip visits Plymouth voluntarily and denies his involvement in the death of Sassamon.

June 1675

June 1. The trial of the three defendants is held, and they are all found guilty and sentenced to death.
June 8. Tobias and Mattashunnamo are executed.
Wampapaquan's execution fails due to a defective rope.
Between June 8 and 18, the attempt of Deputy Governor John Easton and other leaders of Rhode Island to mediate the conflict between the Wampanoags and Plymouth Colony is made but fails.
June 19. The Wampanoags attack Swansea.
June 28. Swansea is nearly destroyed, and King Philip's War is underway.

July 1675

Wampapaquan is shot to death.
King Philip and his men are forced to leave Mount Hope for the Nipmuck country.

August 1675

On August 1, Philip and his Wampanoags barely escape the English attack at Nipsachuck. The Nipmucks ambush the Massachusetts delegates on a peace mission on August 2 and attack two Massachusetts frontier towns, Brookfield on August 3 and Lancaster on August 22.

September–
December 1675

The combined forces of the Nipmucks, the Wampanoags, and the Narragansetts attack frontier towns, such as Deerfield, Squakeag, and Hadley, of Massachusetts and Connecticut in the upper Connecticut Valley.

October 1675

On October 8, the Narragansetts and the

{ *Igniting King Philip's War* }

United Colonies sign a treaty to maintain peace between them, but the Narragansetts break the terms of the treaty. Ninigret and his Eastern Niantics remain neutral.

November 1675
The United Colonies of New England declares war on the Narragansetts on November 12.

November–December 1675
Philip and his men travel to the Mahican country north of Albany and seek allies and support from them, Canadian Indians, and the French, but their attempts all fail.

December 1675
On December 19, the army of the United Colonies attacks and destroys the Narragansett fort in the Great Swamp. Nearly 1,000 Narragansetts—warriors, women, and children—are either killed or captured.

February–March 1676
The Nipmucks concentrate on attacking the Massachusetts frontier towns east of Mount Wachusett: Lancaster, Medfield, and Groton.

February 1676
The Nipmucks capture Mary Rowlandson and others when they attack Lancaster.

April 1676
The Narragansett sachem Canonchet (Nananawtunu) is captured and killed.

July 1676
Philip and a considerable number of the Wampanoags and the Narragansetts return to their own country in the southwestern reaches of Plymouth Colony. Philip's wife and son are captured.

August 1676
On August 12, Philip is killed.

September 1676   Annawon, Philip's most trusted companion and war leader, is captured and executed. King Philip's War ends.

BIBLIOGRAPHICAL ESSAY

Note from the Series Editors: The following bibliographical essay contains the major primary and secondary sources the author consulted for this volume. We have asked all authors in the series to omit formal citations in order to make our volumes more readable, inexpensive, and appealing for students and general readers. In adopting this format, Landmark Law Cases and American Society follows the precedent of a number of highly regarded and widely consulted series.

This essay covers not only the works consulted specifically for this book but also other important studies useful for the understanding of the period and subject matter this book deals with. Although it is not intended to be exhaustive, this essay includes both primary printed materials and secondary works.

On the history of the Plymouth colony, the essential documentary source on its early history is William Bradford, *Of Plymouth Plantation, 1620–1647*. The edition by Worthington C. Ford, 2 vols. (Boston: Massachusetts Historical Society, 1912), contains very extensive annotative footnotes. A more recent and more readable edition is by Samuel E. Morison (New York: Alfred A. Knopf, 1952). Other important sources are George Willison, ed., *The Pilgrim Reader: The Story of the Pilgrims as Told by Themselves and Their Contemporaries, Friendly and Unfriendly* (New York: Reynal and Hitchcock, 1951); Edward Winslow, *Good Newes from New England: or a True Relation of Things Very Remarkable at the Plantation of Plimouth in New-England* (London: 1624) in Alexander Young, ed., *Chronicles of the Pilgrim Fathers of the Colony of Plymouth* (Boston: Little, Brown, 1841), 354–367; *A Relation or Journal of the Beginning and Proceeds of the English Plantation Settled at Plymouth* (London: I. Bellamie, 1622), known as *Mourt's Relation;* Peter C. Mancall, ed., *Envisioning America: English Plans for the Colonization of North America, 1580–1640* (New York: St. Martin's Press, 1995); Glenn W. LaFantasie, ed., *The Correspondence of Roger Williams*, 2 vols. (Hanover, N.H.: Brown University Press/University Press of New England, 1988); Samuel G. Drake, ed., *Old Indian Chronicle . . . and Chronicles of the Indians* (Boston: Antiquarian Institute, 1836); Charles Orr, ed., *History of the*

Pequot War: The Contemporary Accounts of Mason, Underhill, Vincent and Gardener (Cleveland: Helman-Taylor Co., 1897); William Hubbard (minister of the Ipswich church), *A General History of New England*, Massachusetts Historical Society *Collections*, 2nd ser., 5 and 6 (1915); Cotton Mather, *Magnalia Christi Americana; The Ecclesiastical History of New-England; from Its First Planting, in the Year 1620, unto the Year of our Lord 1698* (1702), ed. Thomas Robbins, 2 vols. (New York: Russell & Russell, 1967); and Nathaniel Morton, *New Englands Memoriall* (Cambridge, Mass.: John Usher, 1669). The major public records of Plymouth Colony are Nathaniel Shurtleff and David Pulsifer, eds., *Records of the Colony of New Plymouth*, 12 vols. (Boston: Press of W. White, 1855–1861), especially the first six volumes, which contain court orders.

For a survey of the history of Plymouth, see John G. Palfrey, *History of New England*, 5 vols. (Boston: Little, Brown, 1858–1890) (treats Plymouth in the larger context of New England); Rowland G. Usher, *The Pilgrims and Their History* (New York: Macmillan, 1918); Charles M. Andrews, *The Colonial Period of American History*, 4 vols. (New Haven: Yale University Press, 1934–1938); George Willison, *Saints and Strangers* (New York: Reynal and Hitchcock, 1945); Bradford Smith, *Bradford of Plymouth* (New York: Lippincott, 1951); Samuel E. Morison, *The Story of the "Old Colony" of New Plymouth* (New York: Knopf, 1956); and John Demos, *A Little Commonwealth: Family Life in Plymouth Colony* (New York: Oxford University Press, 1970). The best general account of Plymouth Colony that treats its entire period thoroughly is George D. Langdon Jr., *Pilgrim Colony: A History of New Plymouth, 1620–1691* (New Haven: Yale University Press, 1966).

On Indian-English relations in the Plymouth colony, the first solid analysis, depicting a fair treatment of the Indians by the Pilgrims, is David Bushnell, "The Treatment of the Indians in Plymouth Colony," *New England Quarterly* 26 (1953): 193–218. Alden T. Vaughan, *New England Frontier: Puritans and Indians, 1620–1675* (Boston: Little, Brown, 1965), is one of the most important and thorough studies on Indian-English relations in New England. Challenging the traditional view that the Puritans were often ruthless and unjust in their dealings with the Indians, Vaughan demonstrates that the colonists' treatment of the Indians was fair and just, or at least understandable. Although his focus is the Puritans' side, and his position favorable to them, Vaughan does dip deeply into the Indian side in many aspects of Indian-white relations. The book's two revised editions (W. W. Norton, 1979, and University of Oklahoma Press, 1995) provide lengthy new introductions that reflect his changing interpretations in response to recent studies.

Francis P. Jennings in turn bitterly criticizes the interpretive position established by Vaughan, in Jennings, *The Invasion of America: Indians, Colonialism, and the Cant of Conquest* (Chapel Hill: University of North Carolina Press, 1976), another extensive and masterly treatment of the subject. It analyzes every major event from different angles and severely attacks the actions and motives of the English. Although it is not always convincing, nor does it suggest any definite alternative position, the book does profoundly stimulate and deepen our perspective on the complex nature of Indian-English relations. Still another essential work for the period is Neal Salisbury, *Manitou and Providence: Indians, Europeans, and the Making of New England, 1500–1643* (New York: Oxford University Press, 1982), which provides some sharp ethnohistorical insight into the native side and role in Indian-white relations. Richard Slotkin, *Regeneration through Violence: The Mythology of the American Frontier, 1600–1860* (Middletown, Conn.: Wesleyan University Press, 1973), presents a very exciting psychohistorical account of the Pequot War and King Philip's War.

On the southern New England Indians, a huge number of books and articles have been written. Wilcomb E. Washburn, *The Indian in America* (New York: Harper and Row, 1975), makes numerous references to the New England Indians, while John R. Swanton, *The Indian Tribes of North America* (Washington, D.C.: Smithsonian Institution, 1952), provides a useful guide to the location of Indian villages. Gary B. Nash, *Red, White & Black: The Peoples of Early North America*, 3d ed. (Englewood Cliffs, N.J.: Prentice-Hall, 1992), includes a succinct but insightful treatment of English-Indian relations in early New England. Robert S. Grumet, ed., *Northeastern Indian Lives, 1636–1816* (Amherst: University of Massachusetts Press, 1996), contains a series of biographical essays on major Indian leaders in southern New England. Works in that volume that are especially noteworthy and pertinent to this study are Paul A. Robinson,

"Lost Opportunities: Miantonomi and the English in Seventeenth-Century Narragansett Country," 13–28; Eric S. Johnson, "Uncas and the Politics of Contact," 29–47; John A. Strong, "Wyandanch: Sachem of the Montauks," 48–73; Kevin A. McBride, "The Legacy of Robin Cassacinamon: Mashantucket Pequot Leadership in the Historic Period," 74–92; and Ann Marie Plane, "Putting a Face on Colonization: Factionalism and Gender Politics in the Life History of Awashunkes, the 'Squaw Sachem' of Saconet," 140–165. The following works contain comprehensive coverage of all southern New England tribes: Vaughan, *New England Frontier*; Bert Salwen, "Indians of Southern New England and Long Island: Early Period," in Bruce G. Trigger, ed., *Handbook of North American Indians*, vol. 15: *Northeast* (Washington, D.C.: Smithsonian Institution, 1978), 160–176; Douglas E. Leach, *Flintlock and Tomahawk: New England in King Philip's War* (New York: Macmillan, 1958). The extensive editorial notes and footnotes of LaFantasie, ed., *The Correspondence of Roger Williams*, contain a gold mine of detailed and valuable information about southern New England Indians. Williams's relations with the Narragansetts are fully analyzed in Edmund S. Morgan, *Roger Williams: The Church and the State* (New York: Harcourt, Brace and World, 1967). Alfred A. Cave, *The Pequot War* (Amherst: University of Massachusetts Press, 1996), the most recent and the definitive history of the conflict, covers all the Indian tribes involved in the Pequot War. Eric S. Johnson, "'Some by Flatteries and Others by Threatening': Political Strategies among Native Americans of Seventeenth Century New England" (Ph.D. diss., Department of Anthropology, University of Massachusetts, 1993), is a fascinating study of political strategies and intrigues among the New England Indians.

Studies of narrower focus are John W. DeForest, *History of the Indians of Connecticut* (Hartford: William Jas. Hamersley, 1850); Mathias Spiess, *The Indians of Connecticut* (New Haven: Yale University Press, 1933); Howard M. Chapin, *Sachems of the Narragansetts* (Providence: Rhode Island Historical Society, 1931); William S. Simmons and George F. Aubin, "Narragansett Kinship," *Man in the Northeast* 9 (1975): 21–31; William S. Simmons, "Narragansett," in Trigger, ed., *Northeast*, 190–197; Timothy J. Sehr, "Ninigret's Tactics of Accommodation in Indian Diplomacy in New England,

1637–1675," *Rhode Island History*, 36 (1977): 43–53; Elisha R. Potter Jr., *The Early History of Narragansett* (Providence: Rhode Island Historical Society, 1835); Carroll A. Means, "Mohegan-Pequot Relationships, as Indicated by the Events Leading to the Pequot Massacre of 1637 and Subsequent Claims in the Mohegan Land Controversy," *Bulletin of the Archeological Society of Connecticut* 21 (1947): 26–34; Alden T. Vaughan, "Pequots and Puritans: The Causes of the War of 1637," *William and Mary Quarterly*, 3rd ser., 21 (1964): 256–269; John Menta, "The Strange Case of Nepaupuck: Warrior or War Criminal?" *Journal of the New Haven Historical Society* 33 (Spring 1987): 3–17; John A. Sainsbury, "Miantonomo's Death and New England Politics, 1630–1645," *Rhode Island History* 30 (1971): 111–123. Lawrence M. Hauptman and James D. Wherry, eds., *The Pequots in Southern New England: The Fall and Rise of an American Indian Nation* (Norman: University of Oklahoma Press, 1990), includes several valuable chapters: William A. Starna, "The Pequots in the Early Seventeenth Century," 33–47; Lawrence M. Hauptman, "The Pequot War and Its Legacies," 69–80; Neal Salisbury, "Indians and Colonists in Southern New England after the Pequot War: An Uneasy Balance," 81–95; and Kevin A. McBride, "The Historical Archaeology of the Mashantucket Pequots, 1637–1900," 96–116. For a latter-day Pequot and a Methodist minister, William Apess, see Barry O'Connell, ed. and with an introd., *On Our Own Ground: The Complete Writings of William Apess, A Pequot* (Amherst: University of Massachusetts Press, 1992). William Simmons, *Spirit of the New England Tribes: Indian History and Folklore, 1620–1984* (Hanover, N.H.: University Press of New England, 1986), is a fascinating study of the New England Indians' "spirit" through the natives' folklore between 1620 and 1984. See also Constance A. Crosby, "From Myth to History, or Why King Philip's Ghost Walks Abroad," in Mark P. Leone and Parker B. Potter Jr., eds., *The Recovery of Meaning: Historical Archaeology in the Eastern United States* (Washington, D.C.: Smithsonian Institution Press, 1988): 183–209.

Indispensable for understanding the impact of the English settlements in the Indian country are Laurie L. Weinstein, "Indian v. Colonist: Land Competition in Seventeenth Century Plymouth

Colony" (Ph.D. diss., Department of Anthropology, Southern Methodist University, 1983); Laurie L. Weinstein, "The Dynamics of Seventeenth Century Wampanoag Land Relations: The Ethnohistorical Evidence for Locational Change," *Bulletin of the Massachusetts Archaeological Society* 46, no. 1 (1985): 19–35; Laurie Weinstein-Farson, "Land Politics and Power: The Mohegan Indians in the Seventeenth and Eighteenth Centuries," *Man in the Northeast* 42 (1991): 9–16; Peter A. Thomas, "Contrastive Subsistence Strategies and Land Use as Factors for Understanding Indian-White Relations in New England," *Ethnohistory* 23 (1976): 1–18; Peter A. Thomas, "In the Maelstrom of Change: The Indian Trade and Cultural Process in the Middle Connecticut River Valley, 1635–1665" (Ph.D. diss., University of Massachusetts, 1979). Also important are Catherine Marten, *The Wampanoags in the Seventeenth Century: An Ethnohistorical Survey* (Plymouth, Mass.: Plimoth Plantation, 1970); M. K. Bennett, "The Food Economy of the New England Indians, 1605–75," *Journal of Political Economy* 63, no. 5 (October 1955): 369–397; Howard S. Russell, *Indian New England before the Mayflower* (Hanover, N.H.: University Press of New England, 1980); Christina B. Johannsen, "European Trade Goods and Wampanoag Culture in the Seventeenth Century," in Susan G. Gibson, ed., *Burr's Hill: A Seventeenth Century Wampanoag Burial Ground in Warren, Rhode Island* (Bristol, R.I.: Haffenreffer Museum of Anthropology, Brown University, 1980), 25–33; Salisbury, "Indians and Colonists in Southern New England after the Pequot War," 81–116; William Cronon, *Changes in the Land: Indians, Colonists, and the Ecology of New England* (New York: Hill and Wang, 1983); Kathleen J. Bragdon, "'Another Tongue Brought In': An Ethnohistorical Study of Native Writings in Massachusetts" (Ph.D. diss., Department of Anthropology, Brown University, 1981); Kathleen J. Bragdon, *Native People of Southern New England, 1500–1650* (Norman: University of Oklahoma Press, 1996).

Some histories of the Plymouth towns, such as Bristol, Taunton, Rehoboth, Bridgewater, Marshfield, and Duxbury, are available, but for our purpose Middleborough is the most important. See Thomas Weston, *History of Town of Middleboro* (Cambridge, Mass.: 1906).

During the first forty years of their encounter with the Plymouth colony, the Wampanoags maintained friendly relations, although the Pilgrims' attitudes and policies toward them gradually changed, and the relationship rapidly deteriorated after that. See Vaughan, *New England Frontier;* Langdon, *Pilgrim Colony;* Jennings, *The Invasion of America;* Salisbury, *Manitou and Providence;* and a brief, popular account of Wampanoag-Pilgrim relations, George Howe, "The Tragedy of King Philip," *American Heritage* 10, no. 1 (December 1958): 65–80. For Plymouth's early relations with the Wampanoags, see Bradford, *Of Plymouth Plantation; Mourt's Relation;* Winslow, *Good Newes.* Plymouth Colony's participation in the Confederation of New England and its involvement in Indian affairs throughout New England are recorded in vols. 9 and 10 of Shurtleff and Pulsifer, eds., *Records of the Colony of New Plymouth.*

For the period after the death of Massasoit, see, in addition to the works cited above, *Records of the Colony of New Plymouth,* vols. 4 and 6; Philip Ranlet, "Another Look at the Causes of King Philip's War," *New England Quarterly* 61, no. 1 (March 1988): 79–100; Virginia D. Anderson, "King Philip's Herds: Indians, Colonists, and the Problem of Livestock in Early New England," *William and Mary Quarterly,* 3rd ser., 51 (1994): 601–624. On the ability and leadership of King Philip, little information is available, but his general portrayal may be pieced together from the information presented in the works of Bodge, Leach, Vaughan, Langdon, Jennings, LaFantasie, Howe, and Ranlet.

Historians have written much about the Christianization of the native Americans. For English missionary activities, see William Kellaway, *The New England Company, 1649–1776: Missionary Society to the American Indians* (London: Longmans, 1961); Ola E. Winslow, *John Eliot, "Apostle to the Indians"* (Boston: Houghton Mifflin Co., 1968); Yasuhide Kawashima, "Legal Origins of the Indian Reservation in Colonial Massachusetts," *American Journal of Legal History* 13 (1969): 42–56; Neal Salisbury, "Red Puritans: The Praying Indians of Massachusetts Bay and John Eliot," *William and Mary Quarterly,* 3rd ser., 31 (1974): 27–54; Kenneth B. Morrison, "'That Art of Coyning Christians': John Eliot and the Praying Indians of Massachusetts," *Ethnohistory* 21 (1974): 77–92; James B. Ronda, "'We Are Well as We Are': An Indian Critique of Seventeenth Century Christian Missions," *William and Mary Quarterly,* 3rd ser., 34 (1977): 66–82; William S. Simmons, "Conversion from Indian to

Puritan," *New England Quarterly* 52 (1979): 197–218; James Axtell, *The Invasion Within: The Contest of Cultures in Colonial North America* (New York: Oxford University Press, 1985); James Naeher, "Dialogue in the Wilderness: John Eliot and the Indians' Exploration of Puritanism as a Source of Meaning, Comfort, and Ethnic Survival," *New England Quarterly* 62 (1989): 346–368; Harold W. Van Lonkhuyzen, "A Reappraisal of the Praying Indians: Acculturation, Conversion, and Identity at Natick, Massachusetts, 1646–1730," *New England Quarterly* 63 (1990): 396–428; and a most comprehensive and penetrating study on Natick, Jean M. O'Brien, *Dispossession by Degrees: Indian Land and Identity in Natick, Massachusetts, 1650–1790* (New York: Cambridge University Press, 1997). For John Cotton's unsuccessful attempt at Christianizing the Wampanoags during the period 1667–1675, see Cotton's manuscript journal, in the Massachusetts Historical Society, and Langdon, *Pilgrim Colony*. The most recent and penetrating study on the influence of alcohol on the early American Indians is Peter C. Mancall, *Deadly Medicine: Indians and Alcohol in Early America* (Ithaca, N.Y.: Cornell University Press, 1995).

On early American law, many significant works have recently been done. The best general study is Peter C. Hoffer, *Law and People in Colonial America* (Baltimore: Johns Hopkins University Press, 1992, revised 1998), which covers in a concise manner the English background, the legal system and profession, and substantive and procedural law. For more special studies, see Bradley Chapin, *Criminal Justice in Colonial America, 1606–1660* (Athens: University of Georgia Press, 1983); David H. Flaherty, ed., *Essays in the History of Early American Law* (Chapel Hill: University of North Carolina Press, 1969); George Dargo, *Roots of the Republic: A New Perspective on Early American Constitutionalism* (New York: Praeger Publishers, 1974); Edgar J. McManus, *Law and Liberty in Early New England: Criminal Justice and Due Process, 1620–1692* (Amherst: University of Massachusetts Press, 1993); Peter C. Hoffer and N. E. H. Hull, *Murdering Mothers: Infanticide in England and New England, 1558–1803* (New York: New York University Press, 1981); George L. Haskins, *Law and Authority in Early Massachusetts* (New York: Macmillan, 1960); Edwin Powers, *Crime and Punishment in Early Massachusetts, 1620–1692: A Documentary History* (Boston: Beacon Press, 1966);

N. E. H. Hull, *Female Felons: Women and Serious Crime in Colonial Massachusetts* (Urbana: University of Illinois Press, 1987); David G. Allen, *In English Ways: The Movement of Societies and the Transferal of English Local Law and Custom to Massachusetts Bay in the Seventeenth Century* (Chapel Hill: University of North Carolina Press, 1981); David T. Konig, *Law and Society in Puritan Massachusetts: Essex County, 1629–1692* (Chapel Hill: University of North Carolina Press, 1979); and George L. Haskins, "The Legal Heritage of Plymouth Colony," *University of Pennsylvania Law Review* 110 (1962): 847–859. David D. Hall, John M. Murrin, and Thad W. Tate, eds., *Saints and Revolutionaries: Essays on Early American History* (New York: W. W. Norton, 1984), contains some important essays, including: Gail Sussman Marcus, "'Due Execution of the Generall Rules of Righteousnesse': Criminal Procedure in New Haven Town and Colony, 1638–1658," 99–137; G. B. Warden, "The Rhode Island Civil Code of 1647," 138–151; and John M. Murrin, "Magistrates, Sinners, and a Precarious Liberty: Trial by Jury in Seventeenth-Century New England," 152–206. The laws passed by the Plymouth General Court are recorded in vol. 11 of *Records of the Colony of New Plymouth*; *Book of the General Laws of the Inhabitants of the Jurisdiction of New Plimoth* (Cambridge, Mass.: 1672, 2nd ed. 1685); and William Brigham, ed., *The Compact with the Charter and Laws of the Colony of New Plymouth* (Boston: Dutton and Wentworth, 1836).

The law of the Indians in early America is yet to be studied extensively. One exception is John P. Reid, *A Law of Blood: The Primitive Law of the Cherokee Nation* (New York: New York University Press, 1970), which is a penetrating work on the law of the Indians, in specific reference to the Cherokees. There is no comparable work in the other regions. The law of the Wampanoags and other southern New England tribes is only briefly touched upon in Yasuhide Kawashima, *Puritan Justice and the Indian: White Man's Law in Massachusetts, 1630–1763* (Middletown, Conn.: Wesleyan University Press, 1986); Washburn, *The Indian in America*; Wilcomb E. Washburn, *Red Man's Land/White Man's Law: A Study of the Past and Present Status of the American Indians* (New York: Charles Scribner's Sons, 1971); Marten, "The Wampanoags in the Seventeenth Century"; and Johannsen, "European Trade Goods and Wampanoag Culture in the Seventeenth Century."

Legal studies dealing with the Indians have so far been concentrating on Indian-English relations. Robert A. Williams, *The American Indian in Western Legal Thought: The Discourses of Conquest* (New York: Oxford University Press, 1990), analyzes European legal attitudes toward the American Indians in the entire Western Hemisphere. Studies that focus more specifically on New England are Charles E. Eisinger, "The Puritan Justification for Taking the Land," *Essex Institute Historical Collections* 84 (1948): 131–143; James P. Ronda, "Red and White at the Bench: Indians and the Law in the Plymouth Colony, 1620–1691," *Essex Institute Historical Collections* 110 (1974): 200–215; Ruth B. Moynihan, "The Patent and the Indian: The Problem of Jurisdiction in Seventeenth Century New England," *American Indian Culture and Research Journal* 2 (1977): 8–18; Lyle Koehler, "Red-White Power Relations and Justice in the Court of Seventeenth-Century New England," *American Indian Culture and Research Journal* 3 (1979): 1–31; Kathleen J. Bragdon, "Crime and Punishment among the Indians of Massachusetts," *Ethnohistory* 28 (1981): 23–32; Laurie Weinstein, "Survival Strategies: The Seventeenth Century Wampanoag and the European Legal System," *Man in the Northeast* 26 (1983): 81–86; James W. Springer, "American Indians and the Law of Real Property in Colonial New England," *American Journal of Legal History* 30 (1986): 25–58; and Kawashima, *Puritan Justice and the Indian*.

About the life of John Sassamon not much is known. Bits of information can be gathered from William Hubbard, *A Narrative of the Troubles with the Indians in New-England* (1677), ed. Samuel G. Drake, 2 vols. in 1 (New York: Kraus Reprint Co., 1969); Increase Mather, *A Brief History of the War with the Indians in New-England* (Boston, 1676), and *A Relation of the Troubles Which Have Hapned in New-England, by Reason of the Indians There* (Boston: John Foster, 1677); *Records of the Colony of New Plymouth*, vols. 4, 5, 10, and 12; John L. Sibley, *Biographical Sketches of Graduates of Harvard University*, 3 vols. (Cambridge, Mass.: Charles William Sever, University Bookstore, 1873–1885), vol. 1; Samuel E. Morison, *Harvard College in the Seventeenth Century*, 2 vols. (Cambridge, Mass.: Harvard University Press, 1936); and George M. Bodge, *Soldiers in King Philip's War* (Boston: published by the author, 1891). The most thorough treatment of John Sassamon so far are Jill Lepore, "Dead Men Tell

174   { *Igniting King Philip's War* }

No Tales: John Sassamon and the Fatal Consequences of Literacy," *American Quarterly* 46, no. 4 (December 1994): 479–512 and *The Name of War: King Philip's War and the Origins of American Identity* (New York: Knopf, 1998). For an exciting analysis of Atlantic creoles, see Ira Berlin, *Many Thousand Gone: The First Two Centuries of Slavery in North America* (Cambridge, Mass.: Harvard University Press, 1998).

On the cause of Sassamon's death, most of the contemporary English writers believed that Sassamon had been murdered, but they widely disagreed as to why he was murdered. See, for example, Nathaniel Saltonstall, *The Present State of New-England with Respect to the Indian War* (London, 1675), reprinted in Charles H. Lincoln, ed., *Narratives of the Indian Wars, 1675–1699* (New York: Charles Scribner's Sons, 1913), 24–74; Increase Mather, *A Brief History of the War* and *A Relation of the Troubles;* and Hubbard, *A Narrative of the Troubles.* For a very different view expressed by an English contemporary, see John Easton, *A Relation of the Indian War, 1675* (December 1675), printed in Lincoln, ed., *Narratives of the Indian Wars,* 1–17, in which the author suggests that Sassamon might simply have fallen through the ice and drowned.

Recent historians also disagree with one another. While Douglas Leach in his *Flintlock and Tomahawk* maintains that the evidence is not conclusive enough to determine the guilt of the accused, Langdon in *Pilgrim Colony* seems to assume that Sassamon was murdered and the three accused were indeed guilty of the murder. The most comprehensive and persuasive analysis of the subject is James P. and Jeanne Ronda, "The Death of John Sassamon: An Exploration in Writing New England Indian History," *American Indian Quarterly* 1 (1974): 91–102. The authors examine all the versions of the story of Sassamon's death and recent historians' interpretations meticulously and conclude that Sassamon's death is still a mystery; they call for not only a continuous search for more documentary evidence but, more importantly, a quest for Indian perspectives of the case. For a slightly different view, see Ranlet, "Another Look at the Causes of King Philip's War."

Forensic medicine (medical jurisprudence) in early America is an undeveloped field. A limited amount of information, however, can be gleaned from F. E. Fodere, *Traite de Medicine Legale . . .* , 6 vols.

(Paris: 1813), vol. 3; Theodric R. Beck, *Elements of Medical Jurisprudence*, 2 vols. (Albany, N.Y.: Websters and Skinners, 1823); Robert E. Griffith, "On Medical Jurisprudence," *Philadelphia Journal of the Medical and Physical Science* 10 (1825): 36–46; Stephen Williams, *Catechism of Medical Jurisprudence; Being Principally a Compendium of the Opinions of the Best Writers upon the Subject* (Boston: Hilliard, Gray, & Co., 1835); Edward Marten, *The Doctor Looks at Murder* (Garden City, N.Y.: Doubleday, Doran and Co., 1937); M. N. Stone, "Autochiria: A Seventeenth Century Lawyer on Suicide," *Bulletin of History of Medicine* 14 (July 1943): 173–180; Erwin H. Ackerknecht, "Early History of Legal Medicine," *CIBA Symposia* 2, no. 7 (Winter 1950–1951): 1286–1289; Sidney Smith, "History and Development of Legal Medicine," in R. B. H. Gradwohl, ed., *Legal Medicine* (St. Louis: Mosby, 1954), 1–19; S. K. Niyogi, "Historic Development of Forensic Toxicology in America up to 1978," *American Journal of Forensic Medicine and Pathology* 1, no. 3 (September 1980): 249–264; Jaroslav Nemec, comp., *Highlights in Medicolegal Relations* (Washington, D.C.: U.S. Government Printing Office, 1976); James C. Mohr, *Doctors and Law: Medical Jurisprudence in Nineteenth-Century America* (Baltimore: Johns Hopkins University Press, 1993); Michael Dalton, *The Countrey Justice* (1622) (New York: Arno Press, 1972); *The Conductor Generalis: or, the Office, Duty and Authority of Justices of the Peace* (Philadelphia, 1722; 2nd enlarged ed. 1749); George Webb, *The Office and Authority of a Justice of the Peace* (Williamsburg, Va., 1736); and William R. Brock, *Scotus Americanus: A Survey of the Sources for Links between Scotland and America in the Eighteenth Century* (Edinburgh: Edinburgh University Press, 1982).

The trial of the three Wampanoags is not fully and accurately documented. The official records provide only sketchy information on the trial in *Records of the Colony of New Plymouth*, vol. 5. Some secondary works by Bodge, Leach, Langdon, Jennings, and Lepore do mention the case, but only briefly. We don't even know how long the trial lasted, although we may suspect that it lasted more than one day.

Nor are Indian voices truly heard in the records. Those natives who had mastered English, such as John Sassamon and James Printer, did not write their accounts for various reasons, though valuable such stories might have been. But all are not lost. John Easton's "A Relacion of the Indyan Warre," for example, contains not only Philip's reaction to Plymouth justice but Easton's pro-Indian views and feelings drawn from Indian opinions, beliefs, and information. The Pequot William Apees's "Eulogy on King Philip," delivered in 1836, reprinted in O'Connell, ed., *On Our Own Ground*, represents one of many Indian views and reactions. Critical historians may hopefully be able to read with a discerning eye even documents written by the English in such a way as to bring about the Indian perspective to the story.

On the nature of King Philip's War from the technological and tactical point of view, several important studies have been made. While Douglas Leach's article, "The Military System of Plymouth Colony," *New England Quarterly* 24 (1951): 342–364, is a useful survey of the Plymouth colony militia system, John K. Mahon's "Anglo-American Methods of Indian Warfare, 1676–1794," *Mississippi Valley Historical Review* 45 (1958): 254–275, discusses the difficulty that men who were accustomed to the European terrain had in learning to fight in the American forest. See also Adam Hirsch, "The Collision of Military Cultures in Seventeenth Century New England," *Journal of American History* 74 (1988): 1187–1212; Patrick M. Malone, "Changing Military Technology among the Indians of Southern New England, 1600–1677," *American Quarterly* 25 (1973): 48–63; and Patrick M. Malone, *The Skulking Way of War: Technology and Tactics among the New England Indians* (Lanham: Madison, 1991).

The causes of King Philip's War are diverse and complex. For contemporary accounts of the causes of the war, see the writings of John Easton, William Hubbard, and Increase Mather already cited above and A. B. Hart, ed., *American History Told by Contemporaries*, 5 vols. (New York: 1897–1929), I. For recent interpretations of the causes of the war, see Bodge, *Soldiers in King Philip's War*; Leach, *Flintlock and Tomahawk*; Vaughan, *New England Frontier*; Langdon, *Pilgrim Colony*; and Jennings, *The Invasion of America*.

On King Philip's War itself, there are a number of contemporary accounts. See Lincoln, ed., *Narratives of the Indian Wars*, which contains Easton, "A Relacion of the Indyan Warre," 3–23, Mary Rowlandson, "Narrative of the Captivity of Mrs. Mary Rowlandson," and Saltonstall's three essays, 24–99; Hubbard, *A Narrative of the Troubles with the Indians in New England*; Increase Mather, *A Brief History of the War with the Indians in New-England*; Thomas Church,

Entertaining Passages Relating to Philip's War Which Began in the Month of June, 1675 (Boston: B. Green, 1716) (written later by the son of Captain Benjamin Church but verified by him before he died); Douglas E. Leach, ed., *A Rhode Islander Reports on King Philip's War: The Second William Harris Letter of August, 1676* (Providence: Rhode Island Historical Society, 1963); Daniel Gookin, "An Historical Account of the Doing and Suffering of the Christian Indians in New England, in the Years of 1675, 1676, 1677," *Transactions and Collections of the American Antiquarian Society,* 2 (1836): 429–534; Cotton Mather, *Magnalia Christi Americana;* Jenny Hale Pulsipher, "Massacre at Hurtleberry Hill: Christian Indians and English Authority in Metacom's War," *William and Mary Quarterly,* 3d ser., 53 (1966): 459–486.

Among many secondary works on King Philip's War, the following are the most important: Bodge, *Soldiers in King Philip's War,* contains not only the rosters of the various Massachusetts companies and many Massachusetts Archives documents but also much valuable information in its introduction and last several chapters. Douglas Leach, *Flintlock and Tomahawks,* the definitive study on King Philip's War, is based upon exhaustive research, and continues to be the standard work on the subject. Wilcomb E. Washburn, "Seventeenth-Century Indian Wars," in Trigger, ed., *Northeast,* 89–100, is a concise, crisp essay on King Philip's War in the context of all the Indian wars in the colonies. The most recent study on the war is James D. Drake, *King Philip's War: Civil War in New England, 1675–1676* (Amherst: University of Massachusetts Press, 1999), which examines the diverse, conflicting groups among the English and the natives and treats the war in multiple perspectives.

The impact of the war on the Plymouth colony, including the treatment of Indian captives, can be seen in the *Records of the Colony of New Plymouth,* vols. 5 and 11. For the colonists' reaction to the war, see Richard Slotkin and James K. Folsom, eds., *So Dreadful a Judgment: Puritan Responses to King Philip's War, 1676–1677* (Middletown, Conn.: Wesleyan University Press, 1979).

Post-1676 English-Indian relations, which had long been neglected, have been receiving considerable attention from scholars in recent years. The following studies reflect a variety of topics to which scholars have been attracted: John A. Sainsbury, "Indian

Labor in Early Rhode Island," *New England Quarterly* 48 (1975): 378–393; Richard R. Johnson, "The Search for a Usable Indian: An Aspect of the Defense of Colonial New England," *Journal of American History* 64 (1977–1978): 623–651; Laura E. Conkey, Ethel Boissevain, and Ives Goddard, "Indians of Southern New England and Long Island: Late Period," in Trigger, ed., *Northeast*, 177–187; Kawashima, *Puritan Justice and the Indian*; Kawashima, "Legal Origins of the Indian Reservation"; Daniel Mandell, "'To Live More Like My Christian English Neighbors': Natick Indians in the Eighteenth Century," *William and Mary Quarterly*, 3rd ser., 48 (1991): 552–579, and *Behind the Frontier: Indians in Eighteenth-Century Eastern Massachusetts* (Lincoln: University of Nebraska Press, 1996); Jack Campisi, "The Emergence of the Mashantucket Pequot Tribe, 1637–1975," in Hauptman and Wherry, eds., *The Pequots in Southern New England*, 117–140, and "The New England Tribes and Their Quest for Justice," ibid., 179–193; William S. Simmons, "The Mystic Voice: Pequot Folklore from the Seventeenth Century to the Present," ibid., 141–178; Paul R. Campbell and Glen W. LaFantasie, "Scattered to the Winds of Heaven: Narragansett Indians 1676–1880," *Rhode Island History* 37 (Aug. 1978): 67–83; Laurie Weinstein, "'We're Still Living on Our Traditional Homeland': The Wampanoag Legacy in New England," in Frank W. Porter III, ed., *Strategies for Survival: American Indians in the Eastern United States* (Westport, Conn.: Greenwood Press, 1989), 85–112; O'Brien, *Dispossession by Degrees*; and Colin G. Calloway, ed., *After King Philip's War: Presence and Persistence in Indian New England* (Hanover, N.H.: University Press of New England, 1997).

INDEX

Body of Liberties of Massachusetts
of 1641, 104–105
Bologna, Italy, 89
Boston, Mass.
Alexander's plan to vist, 53
Massasoit visits, 52
Miantonomo summoned to, 114
Miantonomo visits, 21–22
Narragansetts sign treaty at, 21
Nipmucks executed on Boston
Common, 115
Pequots' scalps sent to
Massachusetts governor in,
12
Bradford, William, governor of
Plymouth Colony, 45, 62
Bradstreet, Samuel, 78
Breach of agreement, 68
Brewster, Plymouth, 45
Bridgewater, Mass., 45
Bristol, R.I., 51
Brockton, Mass., 30
Broken neck, as forensic evidence
Increase Mather's remark on
Sassamon's, 96–97, 122
Wampanoags' reaction, 122
Brookfield, 133–134
Bruises, as forensic evidence, 96

Callicott, Richard, 76, 77
Canada, 148, 149
Canonchet (Nananawtunu,
Saccohan), Narragansett
principal sachem
captured and executed, 115,
138–139
his army defeated, 138
importance of corn to his people,
38, 138
plan to attack the English,
142–143
son of Miantonomo, 21, 38, 115,
135, 138–139

Canonicus, Narragansett principal
sachem, uncle of Ninigret and
Quaiapen, 21, 22, 26, 28, 124
Cape Cod, 31, 33, 42
Indians (Nausets), 30
Pokanoket villages on, 33
"Capt. Amos," Wampanoag
military leader, joins the pro-
English Indians, 57
"Careswell," Governor Josiah
Winslow's house in
Marshfield, Plymouth, 85
Carver, John, governor of
Plymouth Colony, 115–116
Cassassinnamon, Robin, Pequot
"governor" after Pequot War,
27
Catapazat, son of the Pequot
"boernor" Harmon Garrett
cremates Canonchet's body,
139
in Great Swamp fight, 144
Cattle and swine
English, 48, 63
Indian, 49
Central Falls, R.I., Captain Pierce
defeats Canonchet, 138–139
Chachucust Neck (Indian locality),
42
Charles River, 137
Charlestown, R.I., 143
Chelmsford, Mass., 147
Chief (principal) sachem. See under
Sachem
Chippinoqutt Pond, 42
Christian Indians, 2, 33, 48, 52, 61,
62, 85, 86, 107, 146, 147
as jurors in Sassamon murder
trial, 107
on Martha's Vineyard, 62
as sachems, 61
and tribute to sachem, 48
Wampanoags, 33

Christianization, 61, 76, 133, 143, 156
  and Indian way of life, 61
  of Nipmucks, 133
  opposed by Ninigret, 143
  opposed by Philip, 79–80
  opposed by Uncas, 80
Church, Benjamin, 84, 140–141
Church, Richard, 110
Citizens, Indians as, 154
Civil War, 153
Clans. *See* Indian, clans of the village
Cochenoe, a Montauk Indian servant of Collicott, 77
Coexistence, 72
  legal, 116, 117, 125, 153
Cole, Hugh, Philip's close friend, 55
Commissioners of the United Colonies. *See* New England Confederation
Concealment of murders, Algonquian law of homicide and, 123
Concord, Mass., where Groton settlers took refuge, 138
Coneconan, sachem of Manomet, 56
Conflict of law
  in English-Indian relations, 112–113
  among European nations, 112
Connecticut
  army, 143
  General Court, 90, 142, 145
  militia, 138
  Mohegans' reliance on, 145
  support from, during Pequot War, 4
Connecticut River, 13, 28
Connecticut Valley, 13, 15–16, 28
  King Philip's War spreads to, 132–136

Conspiracies, rumors of Indian, ix, 1–2, 24, 28, 35, 120
Constable, in Middleborough, 88, 89, 91, 92, 99
Contusions (ecchymoses), 96, 99, 100
Conversion to Christianity. *See* Christianization
Corbitant, sachem of Mattapoisett, 55
Cornman, Eastern Niantic leader, 136
Coroner, 89, 91, 93, 98
Coroner's inquest, 89, 91, 93, 98. *See also* Jury of inquest
Coroner's jury in Middleborough, 99, 121
Cotton, John, 110
Counsel. *See* Lawyers
Counterretaliation among the Algonquians, 68
Court of Oyer and Terminer, 110
Crimes without victims, under New England Indian law, 68
Cromwell, Oliver, 28
Cross-examination, 105
"Cruentation," 100
Cultural imperialism. *See* Imperialism
Curfew law, for the Indians, 154
Curtis, Ephraim, 132–133

Dances, in modern powwows, 61
Dartmouth, Mass., land around, sold by Wamsutta, 45
Death penalty, mode of, in New England colonies, 110–111
Death sentences and executions of the three Wampanoag defendants, 109–110
Deed, Indian deed of 1648 of Plymouth, 46

Extraterritoriality, 66
Extraterritorial rights, 116

Face, appearance of, as forensic
    evidence, 97
Fairs, in modern powwows, 61
Fear of Indians, 2, 120
Felix, husband of Betty (Sassamon's
    daughter), 81
Felony defendants, and right to
    counsel, 105
Fences, 48, 63, 127–128
    colonial policy, 127–128
    English law, 127
    Plymouth law, 128
Festivals, as part of modern
    powwows, 61
Fish and fowl, as Indian game, 35
Flintlock, 151
Florence, Italy, 89
Forensic medicine
    in America, 90–91, 125
    in England, 90
    in France, 89
    in Germany, 89–90
    in Italy (Popes' legislation), 89
Forest land, 47
Fornication or "unnatural vice," in
    the Algonquian legal culture, 68
Fort Mystic. See Mystic Fort
Fowl, 38
Fox, 38
Fractures, as forensic evidence, 96
French and Canadian Indians,
    Philip's failure to gain support
    of, 56
Fur trade, 44, 74

Gardener, Lion, Commander of
    Saybrook fort, 4
Gardener's Saybrook fort, 15
Garrett, Harmon (Caushawashott),
    27, 139

Catapazat's father, 139
Pequot governor after the
    Pequot War, 27
Gaseous matters, as forensic
    evidence, 98
Gender roles, among southern
    New England Indians, 59–61
    change in, after King Philip's
    War, 153
Genghis Khan, 150
Genoa, Italy, 89
George, an Indian juror, 107
George, one of Awashonks's
    councilors, 84
Germanic barbarians (tribes),
    100
Glaring mucus, as forensic
    evidence, 93, 94
Gorton, Samuel, 25, 26, 83, 135
Grafton. See Hassanemesit
Greater Wampanoag nation, 64
Great Swamp fight (1675), 136,
    143, 144
Green, Sergeant, one of the
    printers who published the
    Indian Bible in Cambridge,
    146
Groton, Mass., 137–138, 142
Guerrilla warfare, 131, 151
Guilford, Conn., 19, 99
Guns and gunpowder, secured by
    Philip, 84

Hadley, Mass.
    Nipmucks hovering about, 134
    raided by Nipmucks,
        Narragansetts, and
        Pocumtucks, 148
Harris, Richard, 55
Hartford (Wopigwooit), Conn., 4,
    15, 25, 139
Harvard College, 78
    Indian College, 52, 78

Noyes, Rev. James, 146
Nuck-quut-dowaus, chief sachem
    of the Pequots, Uncas's
    ancestor, 17

Obochiguod, Pequot leader of New
    London, 27–28
Oldham, Captain John, 17
Old Queen. *See* Quaiapen
"Old Watuspaquin." *See* Tuspaquin
One-Eyed John. *See* Monoco
Onkus. *See* Uncas
Ordeals by fire and water, 100
Osamequin (Ousamequin). *See*
    Massasoit
Ostracism, 156
Otter, 38
Oweneco, Mohegan sachem and
    father of Uncas, 17
Oweneco, Uncas's oldest son
    his wife and child held as
        hostages, 144
    leads Mohegan firing squad
        which shoots Canonchet, 115,
        139
    leads Mohegans in Great Swamp
        fight, 144
    tried for murdering Narragansett
        sachem Johnequam (1675),
        118–119

Padua, Italy, 89
Pamontaquash (the "Pond
    Sachem"), Wampanoag
    sachem, 42
Paquoag (Indian locality), 134
Paré, Ambroise, French
    medicolegal specialist, 93
Patuckson, the prosecution's sole
    witness in Sassamon case, 100,
    108–109, 121–122
Paturxt ((Plymouth). *See* Plymouth,
    town of; Plymouth Colony

Pawcatuck, a Pequot community
    after King Philip's War, 144
Pawcatuck River, 6, 13, 14, 20, 138,
    139
Peach, Arthur
    case of, 23, 52, 71, 117, 118
    compared with Sassamon case,
        118
    Massasoit attends trial, 52, 117
    mutual agreement among
        Plymouth, Mass., and
        Narragansetts, 117
    trial of, 52, 71
Pennacooks, during King Philip's
    War, 148–149
Penowanganquis, murder victim
    of Peach and his accomplices,
    23
Pequot captives, 77
Pequot Harbour, 11
Pequot "little squaw," Callicott's
    servant, 77
"Pequot maid," Sassamon's wife,
    interpreter for Thomas
    Dudley and Miantonomo,
    77
Pequot (Thames) River, 14
Pequots, 5, 20, 27–28, 138, 144,
    150
Pequot territory, occupied by
    Massachusetts, Connecticut,
    and Rhode Island settlers after
    Pequot War, 27
Pequot War, 4–17, 27, 32, 34, 52,
    143, 149, 150, 151
Personality (jurisdictional concept),
    71, 112, 115, 116, 118
Pessacus (Moosup, Quissucquansh),
    principal sachem of the
    Narragansetts, younger
    brother of Miantonomo, uncle
    of Canonchet, 21, 26, 124,
    135, 139–140

complains young men's leadership undermining his influence, 135
killed by Mohawks, 139–140
Petananuet (or Petonowowett) (Peter Nunnuit), Weetamoo's second husband, 55
Philip (Metacom or Metacomet), Wampanoag chief sachem, son of Massasoit (Osamequin), 1, 24, 32, 33, 39, 42, 45, 47, 51–65, 79, 80, 81, 82, 84, 86–87, 94, 109, 111, 113, 114, 119, 124, 127–132, 133, 136–137, 139–141, 144, 155–156
attitude toward Christianity, 61–62, 79–80
becomes chief sachem, 53
entertains Narragansett sachems, 82, 114
escapes from Nipsachuck and joins the Nipmucks, 57, 131–132
escapes into Weetamoo's Pocasset country, 131
fails to gain support of French and Canadian Indians, 56
fails to get Sassamon's help, 56
grievance of cattle and horses, 127–128
grievance of Christian missionary activity, 127
grievance of Indian testimony, 128
grievance of uncontrolled English settlement, 128–129
haunting by his ghost, 155
horses for, 65
hunting camp near Nemasket (1674), 84
killed, 140–141
land dispute in

Wollomonuppoag (Wrentham), 46–47
land selling practice of, 63
name change, 53
in New York, 136–137
Nipmuck sachem attempts to kill, 56–57
Nipmucks' morale boosted by his presence, 132–133
as political leader, 54–59, 63–65
reaction to guilty verdicts and executions, 105, 109, 111, 119, 124
relations with Sassamon, 86–87
rumor of his plan to help French attack New England, 62
Sassamon serves, 79, 81
signs Taunton Agreement (1671), 59
surprised by Swansea attack, 130
takes oath of loyalty to English, 54
testifies that he had no role in Sassamon's death, 101, 113
Pierce, Capt. Michael, devastates Narragansett force, 138
Pilgrims, 31–33, 41, 42, 49, 51, 66, 116
Piscataqua, 140
Planting season for Algonquians, 37
Plymouth, town of, 23, 31, 51, 129
Pilgrims landed in, 31, 41
reported Wampanoag arming around, 129
Plymouth bill of rights, guaranteed in the Plymouth *Colony Book of General Laws*, (1672), 122
Plymouth *Book of Laws. See* Plymouth bill of rights
Plymouth Colonial Records, 92
Plymouth Colony, 20, 41, 52, 64, 81, 82, 88, 91, 101, 102, 103, 105, 112, 113, 127, 153

{ *Igniting King Philip's War* }

Siciaoggs, band of "River Indians," 148

Soquontamonk (alias "William"), Tuspaquin's son and Wapanoag sachem, 42

Sowams, 37, 45, 51, 53, 54
  Alexander returns and dies, 53
  Massasoit's principal home site and seat of government, sold by Massasoit and Wamsutta, 45

Springfield, Mass., raided by Nipmucks, Narragansetts, and Pocumtucks, 148

Squakeag (Northfield, Mass.), near Paquoag, 134, 142

Squannacook Swamps in Rehoboth, Philip's hunting grounds, 39

State sovereignty, Southerners' assertion of, 153

Stone, Captain John, killed by Sassacus, 15–17

Stone, Rev. Samuel, sudden death of, 90

Stonington, Conn., Canonchet executed at, 139

Strangulation, as forensic evidence, 97

Submersion, as forensic investigation, 98

Sudden death, as forensic investigation, 120

Suicide, as forensic evidence, 93, 95–96

"Summary Procedure," 107

Supreme (chief or principal) sachems, 48. See also Sachem, chief sachem

Swansea, Mass., 45, 59, 110, 129, 132
  attacked by the Wampanoags, 110, 129, 132

Swollen face. See Face, appearance of, as forensic evidence

Swollen head. See Head, swollen, as forensic evidence

Takamunna, Massasoit's third son, 52, 55, 84
  attends Harvard's Indian College, 52
  signs treaty with Plymouth (Nov. 1671), 84

Talcott, Major John, 140

Tatapanum. See Weetamoo

Tatobem, the Pequot principal sachem, 15–17
  held for ransom but killed, 15
  Uncas, descendant of, 17

Taunton, Mass.
  land near, sold by Philip, 45
  Philip signs Agreement of 1671 at, 62
  raided by Wampanoags, 84

Taunton River, 37, 46, 131, 140
  Philip and Weetamoo cross, 131
  right of access to falls for herring run, 46
  Weetamoo drowns in, 140

Territoriality (jurisdictional concept), 66, 71, 102, 112

Thames River, 130, 145

Theft, in Algonquian legal culture, 68, 71–72

Titicut (Indian village), 37

Tobias, 99, 100, 103–105, 109–110, 113, 120–121
  convicted of murdering Sassamon, 109
  faced with insufficient evidence and hostile jury, 121
  hanged, 110
  insists on innocence, 120
  released on bond posted by Tuspaquin and son, 104, 113

comments on Miantonomo's
    death, 25
tries to recall Williams from
    banishment, 22
Winthrop, John Jr., governor of
    Connecticut, 82–83, 119
Wollomonuppoag (Wrentham,
    Mass.), land dispute in, 46–47
Wongunks, "River Indian" band,
    148

Wootonekanuske, Philip's wife and
    Weetamoo's sister, 55
Wopegworrit, chief sachem of
    Pequots and father of
    Tatobem, 17
Wounds, as forensic evidence, 96,
    98
Wussausmon. *See* Sassamon, John
Wyandanch, sachem of Montauks
    on Long Island, 114